CW00535972

Unmasking Freemasonry

Removing the Hoodwink

Selwyn Stevens, Ph.D

PUBLISHED BY

Jubilee Resources International Inc.
PO Box 36-044, Wellington Mail Centre 5045 New Zealand
or our secure Internet Webshop at
www.jubileeresources.org
facebook.com/jubileeresources

ISBN 978-1-877463-00-6

Unless otherwise indicated, all Scriptures are taken from The Holy Bible, New International Version. Copyright 1973, 1978, 1984, International Bible Society. Used by permission.

This book is dedicated to the Saints of God who toil to bring the light of the Gospel of Jesus Christ to people ensnared in the spiritual darkness and deception of secret societies and cults.

The author wishes to acknowledge and thank many people too numerous to mention here who have given advice and encouragement to put this message into print. Your prayer and support have been most valuable, and God's reward awaits you.

Your guarantee of accurate Information: various sources and authorities have been quoted in good faith throughout this book. Every attempt has been made to ensure these quotations are accurate and in context.

CONTENTS

INTRODUCTION

There are many myths about Freemasonry. *(The terms Mason and Freemason are interchangeable.)* Most are promoted by Freemasons themselves; others by those with an antagonistic agenda, and still others by those who have often sensationalised what they haven't fully understood. Sadly, some Christians are guilty of this too.

There are three main reasons why it has been necessary to write this book.

* The first is to inform people about the true nature of Freemasonry from a Bible-based Christian perspective. My challenge to any person reading this book is this; **If something is true then it can stand being questioned, but if it is not true then it needs to be questioned.** I will present evidence which shows that Freemasonry's beliefs and practices need to be questioned.

* The second is to bring to the attention of the wives and families of Freemasons details about the curses and iniquities which have been placed on them, and to provide reliable and proven guidelines to break those curses.

* The third is to show Freemasons what they are really involved in, especially when their own leaders withhold the whole truth. Freemasons must examine the real meaning of their rituals, instead of just boasting about their good deeds. We live in times when people are clamouring for information to allow "Informed Consent." Because it affects our eternal destiny, I believe the spiritual realm must be treated the same way. Sadly, most people are initiated into Freemasonry without enough knowledge of what they are joining. Time will prove that ignorance isn't bliss!

Some Freemasons get very angry when presented with a book such as this, which they perceive (wrongly) to be attacking them and their lodge. Because of this I suggested to readers of the first edition that care should be taken before going to an active Freemason with this book. My real concern is that they may harden their hearts against the truth of the Gospel of Jesus Christ. Despite the above comments, several folk advised me they gave a copy of the book to a family member who was a Lodge member, and many of these men have resigned, and came to an assurance of Eternal Life in Jesus Christ.

Let me say emphatically I do not hate or despise Freemasons. My purpose is not to attack or condemn anyone involved in Freemasonry, but to present information which would cause them to think again, especially if they claim to be a Christian. I have also spoken and corresponded with the families and the men who have held high office in the "Craft." Their advice and encouragement to put this message into print has been unanimous.

WHO ARE THE FREEMASONS?

Few subjects seem to provoke more debate in churches and families than Freemasonry. Few issues divide churches as often as this "Society with secrets" which claims it is not a secret society. I have on file a newspaper article about the Masonic Lodge which described them as "Rotarians with Ritual." These are the people who run retirement homes for the elderly, and who provide study grants for their young people, particularly those orphaned. They fund many community projects for which they delight in seeking publicity, despite often pretending otherwise. Good works are important to them. However most religious and community organisations do good works, so these are not the exclusive domain of Freemasons.

HISTORIC ROOTS

There are many claims about the historic roots of Freemasonry. Some of these are false, and many are embellished to distort the truth. Some Masonic authorities claim a link from the builders of King Solomon's temple, or even to Adam, but there is no credible evidence for either. When we cut through all the myths we find that early Masons were builders and stonecutters for the great temples and cathedrals of Europe during the Middle Ages. Mostly self-employed, they moved from site to site contracting to do the skilled stonework and other construction work. Those free to move about were usually single and were described as the "free" masons.

Much of their construction work was done in workshops and by the 13th century these were called "lodges." Over time these lodges were used increasingly for relaxation and social purposes. Still later they evolved into assemblies of building masons (known as "Operative Masons) who made decisions on employment rights and skill training of their apprentices. As they moved around Europe and beyond, they developed special passwords and handshakes as evidence of their membership of a particular lodge. This was due, in part, because many couldn't read, so papers of introduction or membership were largely useless. Gradually they evolved into a trade guild.

By the 17th century there wasn't the same amount of work around and specialist architects were doing more of it. To maintain the organisational structures they invited non-tradesmen (known as "Speculative Masons") to join, often including the local mayor, sheriff and aristocracy. Gradually, over several decades, these lodges were taken over by these men of influence and learning, many of whom were involved in the religious and political intrigues and subversive movements of the time. This resulted in a significant change of character. During this process, mainly during the late seventeenth century, there was a strong questioning of authority by many people, particularly of the church, due to the corruption of many churchmen at that time. Although many groups sprang up most were driven underground, including the Deists. (Deism is the forerunner of today's Unitarians. They believe that God created the universe and then abandoned it to mankind to make to best of what we could. *"For in Deism, man needs no God, and, in fact, through reason and sacred initiated knowledge, or illumination, Deists believe that man can become as God,"* writes William T. Still.[1] This view differs little from ancient Buddhism or modern New Age occultism.) Most of the modern secrecy of Freemasonry originated from these underground beliefs and the need to avoid suppression by the government and church authorities.

Among those who joined Freemasonry were men such as Francis Bacon, Sir Christopher Wren, Robert Fludd, and many others who belonged to esoteric/ occultic secret societies such as the Rosicrucians and the Illuminati. It was primarily through such men that much of modern Speculative Freemasonry's ritual was put in place. There is strong evidence of the influence of groups and beliefs such as the Knights Templar (an early order of chivalry which became corrupted by their wealth and power, and which was suppressed by order of the Pope), Swedenborgism (a form of spiritism), Gnosticism (a heretical belief confronted by the early Christian Church), the Kabbala (an occult book), Hermeticism, Neoplatonism and then later by the Rosicrucians, the Illuminati and the Theosophical Society. These last three were secret esoteric societies with pretensions of world domination by a political and religious elite. Some falsely allege that Freemasonry came from only one stream of thinking or organisation. Serious historical research reveals that in fact Freemasonry is an amalgam of many such false religions and philosophies.

THE BIRTH OF MODERN FREEMASONRY

Modern Freemasonry was born on June 24, 1717 at the 'Goose and Gridiron Tavern,' when four London lodges formed under Grand Master named Antony Sayer. Individual lodges with rituals did exist much earlier than this. The oldest surviving written lodge Constitution dates from 1480. Others, particularly from Scotland and England, appear to date around 1150 AD. During the 18th century, the Masonic rituals underwent considerable revision to expressly exclude references to Jesus Christ and the God of the Bible. J. S. M. Ward 33[0], one of Freemasonry's major historians, wrote concerning this period, *"A considerable amount of excision was necessitated by the alteration of the clause in the Constitution which changed Masonry from a Christian to a non-Christian basis... Anything Christian was eliminated.*"[2]

This process of removing the Christian content was commenced by Dr. James Anderson and sponsored by Rev. Dr. John Theophilus Desaguliers, the third Grand Master, who held office between 1723 and 1738. This work was completed by the freethinking Deist Grand Master, the Duke of Sussex, around 1813. This included removing all reference to Jesus Christ and introducing the mythical story of the long-lost name of God. The bloody oaths to maintain secrecy were also added to the initiation rites at this time. There has been little significant change since then. The evidence of their own historians shows that Freemasonry abandoned any pretence of a Christian foundation almost 200 years ago. The higher degrees, such as the Ancient & Accepted (sometimes known as the Scottish and York Rites) developed alongside but were not always recognised by the various Grand Lodges. These have since been recognised.

Freemasonry was introduced into France in 1721, Spain in 1728, the United States in 1730, the Netherlands in 1731, Germany in 1733, Canada in 1841, and then throughout much of Europe, South America and beyond. Growth was mushroom-like. One interesting example was that six different national Grand Lodges had established daughter lodges in China by 1788.

There is evidence that Frederick the Great of Prussia, disturbed by the military alliance between France and Austria, joined Freemasonry and had himself installed as the Prussian Grand Master. He then used lodge members to undermine the Monarchy and the Catholic Church in France. This plotting worked very well, ultimately resulting in the French Revolution. One indication of this connection is the use of the Prussian double-headed eagle on the insignia of the Supreme Council of the 33°. (See certificate on page 34)

There is some evidence that Portuguese Freemasons used the same methods to undermine and overthrow their monarchy and bring about the revolutions between 1910 and 1921 which also established a republic. There are even claims, with some evidence, which point to the role played by Freemasons in bringing about the first Russian Revolution in 1917, and the later Spanish revolution. Russian Bolsheviks banned Freemasonry after the second revolution. One Masonic Encyclopaedia I consulted[3] mentioned how Freemasons joined together to help overthrow Emperor Maximillian of Mexico, and it went on to explain that almost all Mexican leaders since then have been Freemasons. Similar statements were made of much of Central and South American countries.

LODGE STRUCTURE

Perhaps you are wondering what all these degrees are about. The charts on the following pages will help. The first three degrees (or steps) of Freemasonry everywhere in the world are known as The Blue Lodge. There are only minor wording and action differences between Blue Lodges in most parts of the world. Those in lower degrees usually have no idea what goes on in the degrees above theirs, and many don't even know they exist.

Above the Blue Lodge there are four main streams or branches. First and oldest is the British Commonwealth stream. Admission to higher degrees is by invitation only, and this accounts for about one-third of all Master Masons. Usually the first step above 3° is the Holy Royal Arch. A few follow up the 'York Rite' structure, but most who are deemed worthy of further elevation tend to go next to the 'Ancient & Accepted' or 'Scottish Rite,' to the Knight Rose Croix or 18°, after which they will next be invited to the 30° followed by 31° and 32°. A select few are admitted into the honorary 33°. Many of the other degrees and orders are only symbolic or honorary and are not operated.

Two other streams exist in the United States of America only. It is now possible for American Master Masons to go to one of the various temples around the country, such as in Washington or Indianapolis, and with the right payment and a good memory they can advance all the way from 3° to 32° in a couple of weekends. This advancement then enables them to enter the Shriners or any of the higher side orders. Due to an obvious racist slant by many Lodge members, (because of a cross-involvement with the Ku Klux Klan) Negroes/ African Americans have established their own Lodge structure, called Prince Hall Freemasonry. It is a duplicate of the white Lodges in virtually every aspect, although it lacks official recognition by them.

The fourth stream is called Grand Orient, and is the most occultic stream of Freemasonry. These are mostly to be found in France, Italy, some other southern European countries plus most of Central and South America, almost exclusively known as Catholic countries.

Over time considerable differences grew between British Grand Lodge and those of the Continent, primarily the Grand Orient Lodge of France (which appears to have had strong Jacobite connections). Fundamentally, Grand Orient Lodges are Atheistic, while Grand Lodges from England and America (and those affiliated with them) are Pantheistic in spiritual or religious beliefs. There remains both competition and an antagonistic distance between the Grand Orient and the other Grand Lodges. Grand Orient removed the necessity of members having a belief in a Supreme Being, and later admitted women as

Blue Lodge Masonic Structure

Local

→ 1^0 - Entered Apprentice → 2^0 - Fellow Craft → 3^0 - Master Mason

(under a "Worshipful Master" & other officers, including Past Masters, Director of Ceremonies, Chaplain, Senior & Junior Wardens, Senior & Junior Deacons, Stewards, Director of Music, Secretary, Treasurer, Inner Guard, & a Tyler, (who stands guard with a sword outside the lodge door when it meets)

Provincial/District
Senior officer is Provincial Grand Master,
(then) Deputy or Assistant P. Grand Master,
(then) other officers responsible for lectures,
finance, secretary, charity (Almoner) etc.
(The P.G.M. functions much like a bishop in an
Anglican/Episcopal structure; the other positions are
his assistants. Also countries such as Australia do not
operate the provincial structure, since each
State/Province has its own Grand Lodge.)

Research Lodge, (some local lodges also have these.)

National or State
Senior officer is Grand Master,
(then) Deputy or Assistant Grand Master,
(then) Senior & Junior Grand Wardens,
(then) other officers responsible for lectures,
finance, secretary, charity (Almoner) etc.
(There may be hundreds, even thousands, of Blue Lodges under a Grand Lodge.
e.g. New Zealand has 300, England over 9,000, Australia 2000, etc.
There is a separate, self-governing Grand Lodge in every state in Australia and
the USA, and every province in Canada. Worldwide there are over
30,000 Blue Lodges, & 100 Grand Lodges or Grand Orients)

NB All this structure is for the Blue Lodge only.

Grand Research Lodge

members of some lodges, including the leaders of the Theosophical Society; Helena P. Blavatsky, Alice Bailey and Annie Besant, who all reached 33°. The Grand Orient developed into an association of freethinkers and atheists with significant occultic tendencies. Following this, a number of national Grand Lodges affiliated with the French Grand Orient, including the Dutch, Turkish, Portuguese, Spanish, Greek, Italian, and those in Belgium, Brazil, Peru, Haiti, Guatemala and Central and South America.

All Masonic Lodges are required to recognise all the others and affiliate with the English Supreme Council. There are so many side degrees, orders and affiliated lodges that most of their own members do not understand all the links. Some Masonic authorities record almost one thousand different degrees, as many national Grand Lodges or Grand Orients have their own unique degree systems beyond the usual Blue Lodge and A & A/Scottish and York Rites. Many titles are taken from long-ceased chivalry orders, while others appear to be pompous and self-glorifying.

Lodge membership seems to be decreasing in most countries. For example, New Zealand's Grand Lodge has lost half its membership of 30 years ago, and over one-third have resigned in seven years. Members are ageing and younger men are either uninterested or know why to stay out. In common with many organisations today, some Freemasons are seeking to adapt the Lodge so it will appear more relevant and (they hope) more popular, while traditionalists are resisting any change. In addition, many Freemasons are being taught the truth about their lodge by Christians, resulting in significant numbers renouncing the ritual and religion of their lodge in favour of a relationship with God through Jesus Christ.

WORLD STRUCTURE

The most important Supreme Councils are:

"Supreme Council of the 33° of the Ancient and Accepted Rite of Heredom for **England and Wales** and its Chapters overseas." (This includes the higher degrees, up to the 33°, operated in most British Commonwealth countries, including New Zealand, Australia, Canada, India, Malaysia, South Africa.)

"Mother Supreme Council of the World of the 33rd and last degree of the Ancient and Accepted Rite of Freemasons - **Southern Jurisdiction**," (based in Washington, D.C., and responsible for a significant part of the rest of the world's higher degrees and orders. This appears to be the most senior of the Supreme Councils, certainly in terms of numbers and influence).

British Commonwealth Masonic Structure

Ancient & Accepted or Scottish Rite

York Rite

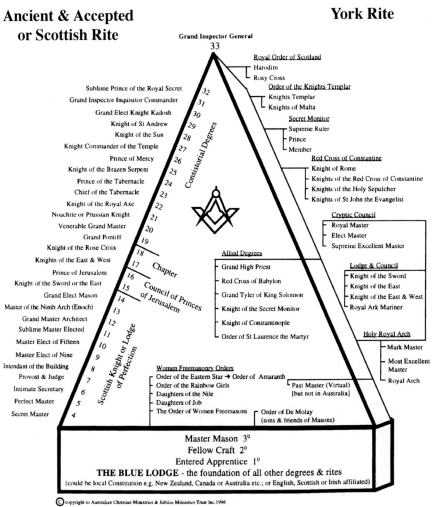

(This is the structure in use in Australia and New Zealand, and is very similar to that used in other countries. Because each is self-governing in most of these degrees and orders, there are some differences but these are usually minor, including titles.)

American Masonic Structure

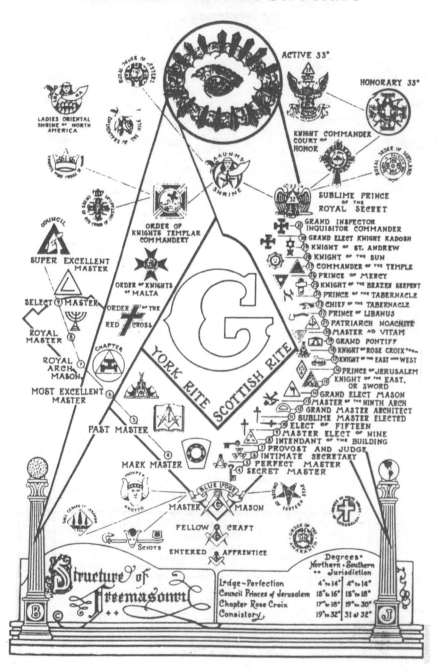

"Supreme Council of the World of the 33rd and last degree of the Ancient and Accepted Rite of Freemasons - **Northern Jurisdiction,**" (based in Boston, USA, responsible for fifteen states, each with it's own Grand Lodge).

"**Scottish** Supreme Council for the Ancient and Accepted Rite of Freemasonry," controls all 33 degrees, similar to the English Supreme Council but including Blue Lodges in various parts of the world, due to movement of Scottish Regiments of the British Army during the 18th and 19th centuries. It has a higher proportion of Roman Catholic members. It also controls the Knights Templar and Knights of Malta degrees, and the Royal Order of Scotland degree. It is based in Edinburgh.

"Supreme Grand Lodge of Free and Accepted Masons of **Ireland**" includes a Supreme Council, and is strongly Protestant. Based in Dublin but strongest in Ulster; similar to the English Supreme Council, although it also controls a number of Blue Lodges in many parts of the British Commonwealth. This arose through the movement of Irish Regiments of the British Army during the 18th and 19th centuries. The Irish Council doesn't work many of the side degrees such as Secret Monitor, Cryptic Council, etc.

There are several dozen Supreme Councils throughout the world. These should not be confused with the various Grand Lodges which govern the lower degrees. All Supreme Councils are constituted under the jurisdiction of the Supreme Council of England and Wales; they must abide by the World Constitution which is administered from there; and others are not permitted to have any degree above their Ancient and Accepted Rite's 33°.

THE SHRINERS

The Shriners are an order unique to North America, with membership limited to those who have reached the 32° Scottish Rite or Knights Templar in the York Rite. On first reading of their initiations one might be forgiven for thinking it is a rude hoax or a tasteless  joke. However there is evidence that the 600,000 American men who belong to this order actually do participate in mock hangings, mock beheadings, mock drinking of the blood of the victims, and having a mock dog urinate on the blindfolded initiate, among other disgusting activities. This degree has been described by Christian author, Walton Hannah, as *"retarded adolescence,"* and I tend to agree. During their ritual, Allah (the god of Islam) is called "the god of their fathers," so Jews, Christians and adherents of other religions couldn't possibly be members, or their declaration invokes a change of religion.

Affiliated Masonic Organisations

Name of Order	Begun	Who may join	Purposes
The Ancient Arabic Order of the Nobles of the Mystic Shrine	1872	American & Canadian men only, those in 32^0 or Knights Templar.	Claimed fund-raising for charity, especially children hospitals, burn units. Also much socialising.
Prince Hall Freemasonry	1784	American Black/ Negro men - most are barred from joining white lodges.	Same as American White Freemasonry but not recognised by it.
Order of the Eastern Star	1850	Wives of Masons worldwide.	Rituals similar to men's lodge, only 5^0 plus philanthropic works
Order of the White Shrine of Jerusalem	1884	Similar to Eastern Star, but USA only.	Charity fund-raising
Order of Amaranth	1873	Masons & all female relatives of all ages. Mainly USA, but branches elsewhere.	Rituals, to 3^0 Royal Court-type ceremonies Moral & religious instruction.
Order of De Molay	1919	White males, 14-21 years, worldwide.	Recruiting ground for men's lodge, also accent on patriotism/morality.
Daughters of the Eastern Star	1925	White females 14-21 yrs. father must be Mason or mother in Eastern Star. USA only.	Rituals to 3^0
International Order of Job's Daughters	1920	White girls, 11-20 yrs. must have relative in Masonic Lodge or Eastern Star. Worldwide.	Secret Rituals, also moral and spiritual guidance. Community fund-raising loans for higher learning
International Order of Rainbow Girls	1922	White females 11-20 yrs. candidates must be recommended by Mason or Eastern Star.	Ritual & symbolism plus 7 stages of initiation.

Most of the above groups have ten to one hundred thousand members each. Prince Hall has over a quarter of a million,; Shriners have 600,000 members, & Eastern Star claim over 3 million. There are also many college fraternities with masonic links, and a number of other minor affiliated orders.

OTHER LODGES AND SECRET SOCIETIES

The **Independent Order of Oddfellows** was established by Freemasons.[4] Like its parent, members of this society are forbidden to pray in the name of Jesus, and their Sovereign Grand Lodge of the World has decreed that
Christianity is only a sect like all other religions. Their rules prohibit the mention of Christianity inside the lodge, claiming this would offend members who are Jews, Moslems and other religions. Like its parent body, members are required only to have a belief in a "supreme being". They also have a Women's auxiliary called the International Association of Rebekah Assemblies.

The **Loyal Order of Orange** professes faith in the One True God and in Jesus Christ. The Order was established in 1688 by Dr. Gilbert Burnett, to support the cause of William, Prince of Orange, who later became King William 3rd. William's army defeated King James 2nd of England at the Battle of the Boyne in Ireland two years later.

The Orange Order was formalised in 1794 for "Mutual defence and maintenance of the (Protestant) Constitution" of England. This was believed necessary due to the growth and strength of Roman Catholic and Republican societies, mainly in Ireland during this period. The main force behind the formalising of The Orange Order were Wilson, Winter and Sloan, all known Freemasons, and two were publicans - not an occupation Christians are known for.

The **Knights of Columbus** are under the authority of the Roman Catholic Church for the basic purpose to promote the Catholic faith. Founded in 1882 in Connecticut, USA, this order is ostensibly a lay organisation offering insurance benefits. They operate a closed fraternal order which closely mirrors Blue Lodge Masonry (except for the death-curse
oaths, which only occur in their fourth degree) with secret initiation rites, recognition signs, passwords and grips and a commitment to support and protect one another. In some parts of America, Knights of Columbus and Freemasons hold joint social meetings, and some Catholic men belong to both groups.

Their first three degrees do not have bloody death oaths like the Freemasons, but there is a focus on promising to keep secrets, loyalty to their church and order, etc. To betray the order is regarded as betraying their church.

Knights of Columbus have about 1.6 million members worldwide.

THE MORMON CONNECTION

It is no coincidence that Masonic oaths, penalties etc. (often word for word) are found in Mormon Temple ceremonies, and particularly in their Aaronic and

THE CHURCH OF
JESUS CHRIST
OF LATTER-DAY SAINTS

Melchizedek Priesthood rites. I have heard Mormons claim that Freemasons must have stolen their ceremonies. Actually the opposite is true. Joseph Smith Jnr. and his brother Hyrum were both Freemasons for some time. There are various views of what happened, but most agree on the main points. Far from keeping the secrets of Freemasonry, Joseph taught them to his followers in early May 1844 and claimed they were "divine revelation."[5] By the end of June both Joseph and Hyrum had been killed in a Western-style gun battle while attempting to escape from Carthage gaol. The Smith brothers were in gaol for burning down a newspaper office which had printed some damaging evidence about the Smith's polygamy and other socially unacceptable behaviour. Waite's Masonic Encyclopaedia records that during 1844 the Grand Lodge of Illinois expelled Brigham Young and over 1500 other Mormons. It raises the interesting question of whether or not the Masonic penalties were enforced to prevent further disclosure. The Masonic Square and Compass are on Mormon Temple veils, on each breast of the sacred undergarments - even the handgrips are the same. This isn't a coincidence.

THE ILLUMINATI

This organisation was founded on May 1st, 1776, by Adam Weishaupt. He was educated by the Jesuit Order. His original goal was to establish a Protestant organisation to fight Jesuitism by using Jesuit methods. The goal included subverting Freemasonry to its aim of world domination by any and every means.

"Politically speaking, its (The Illuminati) tendencies were republican; religiously it was anti-Christian. It's members were pledged to blind obedience to their superiors, and this was ensured by a strict system of secret confession and monthly reports checked by mutual espionage. After obtaining control of certain Masonic Lodges, Weishaupt and his associates recklessly vaunted their growing power," writes historian Lady Queensborough ("Occult Theocracy" p. 372).

Former Illuminati trainer, Svali, from San Deigo, states, *"The Illuminati is a group that practices a form of faith known as "Enlightenment." It is Luciferian, and they teach their followers that their roots go back to the ancient mystery religions of Babylon, Egypt and Celtic druidism. They have taken what they consider the "best" of each ... and joined them together into a strong occult discipline." In 1996 "... when I left the Illuminati, approximately 1% of the US population was either a part, sympathetic, or a victim of mind control" of the Illuminati."*

In the Illuminati, there are three classes of Adepts, with three degrees in each.

Nursery: Preparation Novice: Minerval: & Illuminatus Minor.

Masonry: Symbolic Apprentice, Fellow Craft & Master Mason; Illuminatur Major or Scotch Novice; & Illuminatus Dirigins or Scotch Knight.

Mysteries: Priest/Prince/Regent; Magus or Philosopher & Rex/King (Homme Rei or Areopagite.

The following quotation is most illuminating: *"Freemasonry is a fraternity within a fraternity - an outer organisation concealing an inner brotherhood of the elect ... the one visible and the other invisible. The visible society is a splendid camaraderie of 'free and accepted' men enjoined to devote themselves to ethical, educational, fraternal, patriotic and humanitarian concerns. The invisible society is a secret and most august fraternity whose members are dedicated to the service of a mysterious arcannum arcandrum (secret mystery)."* Manly P. Hall, "Lectures on Ancient Philosophy" p. 433. Hall was Freemasonry's greatest philosopher, according to the Scottish Rite Journal, September 1990.)

College Fraternities and Sororities

These are found widely throughout North America and beyond. Their names consist of two or three Greek letters, such as: Kappa Alpha, Chi Psi, Sigma Chi, Phi Delta Phi, Nu Sigma Nu, Delta Sigma Delta, Delta Sigma Theta, Zeta Tau Alpha, and so on.

The oldest is Phi Beta Kappa, established in 1776. There is secrecy, ritual, oaths of fidelity, a grip, a motto, a badge, comradeship and an urge to share values. Most if not all these have been copied from Freemasonry. The hazing or initiation ceremonies are demeaning and sometimes dangerous. The best source for information on these is *"College Fraternities - the Secret Society on Campus"* by David Carrico.

LET'S NAME SOME NAMES!

Freemasons certainly have the powerful and influential among their membership. Among the better known are Mozart, Voltaire, Casanova, Garibaldi, Simon Bolivar, Anton Mesmer, Johann Goethe, Adam Weishaupt, the first two

Napoleons, Samuel Hahnemann, Robert Burns, Henry S. Olcott, Helena P. Blavatsky, Alice Baily, Annie Besant, Charles Taze Russell, Joseph Smith Jnr., Henry Ford, Charles Lindbergh, Douglas MacArthur, John Wayne, J. Edgar Hoover, Norman Vincent Peale, Yassar Arafat, Shimon Peres, Yitzhak Rabin, George Washington, Benjamin Franklin, Richard Nixon, Jimmy Carter, Gerald Ford, Ronald Reagan, George H. W. Bush, (in fact 17 American Presidents have been Masons). It has been claimed that Prince Charles is the first male member of the British Royal family in over 200 years who hasn't joined the Freemasons. Word has it his grandmother prevented him joining.

In countries like New Zealand and Australia it has seemed that only Freemasons are considered for positions such as Governor or Governor General. Former N.Z. Prime Minister and Governor General, Sir Keith Holyoake, filled 16 of 18 cabinet places with Freemasons, including Sir John Marshall and Sir Robert Muldoon. Sir Keith was also a Grand Master of the Lodge and was in part responsible for New Zealand's Government building known as "The Beehive" - a well-known Masonic symbol. Australian Prime Ministers Sir Robert Menzies, Sir William McMahon, Harold Holt, Bob Hawke & John Howard are or were Freemasons. The political, military and business scene is similar in most countries, including Britain, Canada, the USA, Mexico, European, Central & South American, in fact virtually every other nation on earth which doesn't have a Communist-controlled government.

This very incomplete list shows something of the power and influence of Freemasons in our world. The question arises whether many of these men would have reached those prominent positions had they not been Freemasons? The Masonic obligation to give preference to a brother in the lodge must have some effect. Human nature being what it is, some have been 'social-climbing,' ambitious or just greedy for power. The British print media reported during 1998 that one of the Ten Most Wanted criminals in England was installed as Worshipful Master of a London lodge, while at least eight of the lodge members were policemen who took no action to bring their new Master to justice. Other examples of similar preference and corruption were also given.

CAN A CHRISTIAN BE A FREEMASON?

This is one of many questions asked. Many Lodge members claim "Yes, they can". But is this true in fact? I believe this is the wrong question. The most relevant question is, **"Should a Christian be a Freemason?"** After much research I have to state the answer is an emphatic **"No!"** Let us now investigate the evidence, to see why True Freemasonry and True Christianity are mutually exclusive.

OATHS THAT BIND

So, what of these oaths? Jesus Christ was very specific in Matthew chapter 5 verses 33-37 that Christians are not to swear oaths. James 5: 12 confirms this command. Defining a Christian as a believer in, or disciple of, Jesus Christ, and that the Bible is God's inerrant word, on these foundations we must state that no true Christian could take the oaths attributed to (and never denied) by Masonic leaders. The penalty for breaking the secrets at the first initiation, known as the 'Entered Apprentice' degree. *"Binding myself under no less a penalty than that of having my throat cut across, my tongue torn out by its roots, and buried in the rough sands of the sea at low water mark, where the tide ebbs and flows twice in 24 hours, should I ever knowingly or willingly violate this my solemn oath and obligation as an Entered Apprentice Mason. So help me God, and keep me steadfast in the due performance of the same."*

It is known that many British Commonwealth Grand Lodges, and some others over the past decade, have amended these oaths in the Blue Lodge by sanitising the terms about mutilation. Some lodges have substituted or added to the offending phrases with words like: *"... or the no less effective punishment of being branded as a wilfully perjured individual, void of all moral worth, and totally unfit to be received into this worshipful Lodge..."* Accompanying this oath is a special sign. The right hand, with the palm down and the fingers together, begins with the thumb under the left ear. This is drawn quickly across the throat to the right ear, followed by the hand dropped to the side. This action shows the penalty of having the throat cut and the tongue ripped out. *(One other place where this sign and wording may be found is during the Mormon Temple Endowment Ritual for the First Token of their Aaronic Priesthood.)*

The penalty sworn for Fellow Craft or 2° is to have the left breast torn open, the heart plucked out, and given to the wild beasts of the field and the fowls of the air. The sign is to have the right hand cupped over the left breast, drawing it quickly across the body, then dropping the hand to the side. This action is to rip out the heart. *(This is used in the Second Token of the Mormon Aaronic Priesthood, including the oath.)*

The penalty sworn for the Master Mason or 3° is to have his body cut in two, his bowels removed and burned to ashes which are then to be scattered to the four winds of heaven. The sign is to draw the thumb quickly across the

19

waist to the right hip, then drop the hand to the side. This action shows the stomach being ripped open. *(This is used in the First Token of the Mormon Melchizedek Priesthood.)*

The sworn penalty of the Holy Royal Arch Chapter is to suffer loss of life by having his skull smitten off and his brains exposed to the scorching rays of the noontide sun. The Knights Templar swears to have his head struck off and placed on the highest church spire. Every Masonic degree and Order has a similar graphic death and mutilation penalty.

I wonder what the wives of the men who have taken these oaths think about them? Lodge members are forbidden to tell their spouses, family members or spiritual advisors what they have sworn. Regardless of how sincere and earnest these men may be, this oath requires a person to enter an illegal and criminal bond which endorses murder by others if not himself. How can anyone expect God to help him commit such a crime? If he doesn't intend to keep this oath then he is lying and calls on man and God to witness this. Exodus 20:7 states, **"You shall not take the name of the Lord your God in vain, for the Lord will not hold him guiltless who takes His name in vain."**

There can be no doubt that these are potentially suicide and/or murder pacts! When we reflect that the secrets are trivial, why is it necessary for Freemasons to make such drastic oaths? Many Freemasons claim these oaths are merely ceremonial and meaningless in the modern world. Fair comment, but if this is true, why perpetuate them? If the information being kept secret is so wonderful and enlightening, then why isn't it available for everyone to share? Everything in a truly Christian Church is open to all! **Jesus said, " I spoke openly to the world... I said nothing in secret..."** (John 18:20).

BLIND CONTRACTS
When we consider that initiates are only given one line at a time and are not permitted to know in advance what they are going to swear, then these become blind contracts which most courts of law would find to be unfair and not binding. Under false pretences the initiate is required to swear to conceal crimes by other lodge members if the need should arise. I was interested to read that the State of Connecticut passed a law making Masonic oaths illegal, on the basis that they were subversive to public morals, blasphemous, that they were murderous and criminal in intent and if carried out would make those involved conspiracy to murder.

God's Word requires a Christian to

renounce a bad or sinful oath such as this. **Leviticus 5:4-5 shows us that if a person is required to swear something which was hidden prior to the oath-taking, God says we should plead guilty to Him, confess it as sin and totally renounce and repudiate it, preferably publicly. When you have done this God says you are no longer bound by it.** God wants us to know that repentance releases us from such a vow or oath. This is one of the major keys for removing the consequences of the curses invoked by Masonic oaths.

INITIATED INTO DARKNESS

Freemasonry initiations are humiliating affairs. All metal objects are removed, including any wedding ring. (I wonder if they tell their wives this?) The shirt is unbuttoned to expose the left breast (the reason this is done is to ensure the candidate is a male, for no female is permitted to participate in the rituals in most lodges).

First Degree Mode of Preparation

Hoodwinked or blindfolded

6ft cabletow or noose around neck

dagger etc. pressed against naked left breast

Right arm uncovered. All metal removed including wedding ring.

left leg made bare

right heal slipshod

The Candidate prepared for initiation in the 1st degree. Would you like to see your husband, father or son like this?

The right sleeve is rolled up to above the elbow, the left trouser leg is rolled up above the knee; and the right shoe is removed and replaced with a slipper.

A rope noose, called a "cable-tow" is placed around the neck and the initiate is blindfolded. This blindfold is called a "hoodwink." He is introduced by an officer called the Tyler, as "a poor candidate in a state of darkness." *(If this man is a Christian believer, then how can he be described as being in a state of darkness? Jesus Christ is the "**Light of the World**," so a true Christian cannot be in darkness.)* There is a spear, sword, compass point or small ritual dagger (called a poinyard) which pricks the left breast and is aimed at the heart, empowering an evil blood-covenant. What fear and bondage enters a person at such times? *(Please see the Prayer of Renunciation on page 49 for the list.)* Initiations into Wicca (white witchcraft) are amazingly similar, according to testimonies on the video mentioned on page 62, and confirmed to the writer personally by a man who was once a Wiccan High Priest and a 32⁰ Freemason at the same time, without conflict.

It needs to be said that at no point in the first three degrees is the name of Jesus permitted to be mentioned, even in the prayers. The excuse given is that nothing must be done which would offend any lodge member who is Moslem, Hindu, Jewish or of any other religion. The Liturgy of the Scottish Rite of Freemasonry, states *"All the Degrees of Scottish Masonry can be received by good men of every race and religious faith; and any degree that cannot be so received is not Masonry, which is universal, but some other thing, that is exclusive, and therefore intolerant."⁶*

SECRECY AND DECEIT

Freemasons will not speak with a member who has resigned and spoken publicly about their rituals. They believe this person has broken a sacred oath not to share the secrets of the Lodge, and is therefore an untrustworthy person. As most of their ceremonies are now available from public sources, such as libraries, there really are few secrets. One of the criticisms about Freemasonry is that members aren't even allowed to tell their wives or others what goes on in the lodge. They swear oaths never to reveal the secrets of the Lodge to anyone who isn't a member, if you recall. Many wives of Freemasons speak of this wall of secrecy between them and their husbands, which is hardly a Godly intention in marriage. What most people don't realise is that most Freemasons have secrets kept from them as well. Let me quote from Manly P. Hall, 33°, who quoted this from the Liturgy of the Ancient & Accepted or Scottish Rite. He wrote, *"The Blue degrees are but the outer court or portico of the temple. Part of the symbols are displayed there for the Initiate but <u>he is intentionally misled by false interpretations.</u> It is not intended he should understand them, but <u>it is intended that he shall imagine he understands</u> them."⁷* This is saying that deliberate deceit is used on those in the lower degrees by those above them.

While considering this issue, I was able to listen to a radio talk-back with a Grand Master of the Lodge. As the man in charge of his nation's Blue Lodge, a member of 31° A & A Rite and also of Royal Arch, *(explained on pages 8 -13)* he should have had a reasonable understanding of Masonic things. On several occasions during the talk-back this man denied knowledge of proven ritual and objects in the lodge, or rejected the claims as untrue. He denied that a coffin or similar object was used during the 3° initiation. He didn't seem to know two of Masonry's greatest scholars, Dr. Albert Mackey or Albert Pike. There were several other examples, but by the end of the radio programme I was left with an obvious conclusion. Either this Grand Master hadn't attended many Initiations and Installations, had forgotten what occurred, wasn't able to read from any Masonic books; or he was knowledgeable and was deliberately misleading listeners while trying to avoid controversial questions. I thought about this and considered the invidious position this man had put himself in. When we recall the penalties for revealing any "secrets" about the lodge, no wonder this man wanted to avoid invoking those curses upon himself, so I guess it must have been easier to deny things and/or mislead people. What a "No-win" situation. The various degrees claim to teach morality, integrity, honesty etc., yet Freemasons in the lower degrees are deliberately misled by those above them. Anyone who doubts this should check out the charts on pages 11 and 12, and see how many degrees and orders Freemasons in lower degrees are not told about, unless they are deemed 'worthy' to be invited to join them. Why say there are only three degrees, when there are many higher degrees on public record?

Freemasonry doesn't offer anything which really helps the souls of those who dwell in spiritual darkness. *"Not one of the thirty three degrees of Freemasonry contains any spiritual truth worth all the secrecy and curses. The secrecy and curses only serve to hide, deceive and confuse those who would examine Masonry more closely. Masonry takes selected bits of Christianity, but sets them on top of a very anti-Christian foundation."*[30]

THE SPIRITUAL PROBLEM WITH FREEMASONRY

Freemasonry contends that the holy book of every religion should be **"on the level"** with every other holy book. They can then pretend that all the different deities are equal. Freemasons also claim all deities are only different manifestations of the same God. This explains why they accept members from every religion. The diagram on the following page may assist understanding of this problem.

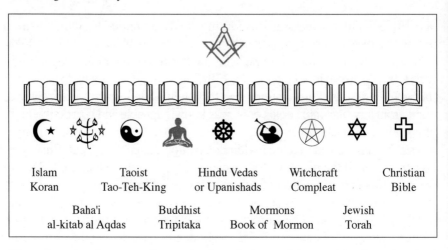

Islam Koran	Taoist Tao-Teh-King	Hindu Vedas or Upanishads	Witchcraft Compleat	Christian Bible
Baha'i al-kitab al Aqdas	Buddhist Tripitaka	Mormons Book of Mormon	Jewish Torah	

Since these books contradict each other, the same deity couldn't have inspired them all, otherwise he could be accused of not knowing his own mind. There's another problem.

* **Buddhism, Taoism, Theosophy and New Age Spiritism teach that everything that exists is God, including oneself;**

* **Hindus & Mormons each have 3 main gods with millions of minor gods, and we each have the potential to become a god too;**

* **Moslems, Baha'i and Unitarians each have a distant, singular god;**

* **Jews & Jehovah's Witnesses both believe God is singular if not so distant;**

* **The God of the Christians is infinite, personal, loving, triune, and He wants a relationship with everyone.**

Any <u>one</u> of the above may be true, but that automatically cancels out the claims of the others because they are contradictory. It is even possible they <u>all</u> may be wrong. Syncretism of these views of deity is impossible - they simply cannot <u>all</u> be right. All but the last of the above views fails to square with the Bible view of deity, and so Christians must reject all the others as false. All through the Bible God warns, (and if that fails He pronounces judgement on) all who worship or follow any other god. The prophet Isaiah records God saying, **"Before Me there was no God formed, nor shall there be after Me... Besides Me there is no God!"** (Isaiah 43:10 & 44:6). If God states there are no other Gods, since He is in a unique place to know we should take His word for it. Also check these Scriptures out for yourself; *Exodus 20:3-5; Numbers 25:1-4; Deuteronomy 12:1-11, 13; Joshua 23:6-7; Isaiah 8:20; Jeremiah 43: 11-13, 44:8; 2 Peter 1:1-2; 2 John 7-10.*

The bottom line is that Freemasonry is misleading people into thinking that all gods are equal when the evidence clearly shows otherwise. This raises a most serious point on which Masonic leaders avoid discussion. **Jesus said "I am the Way, the Truth and the Life; no man comes to the Father but through Me,"** (John 14:6). He is emphatic that there is no way to God which excludes Him, i.e. Jesus Christ. That is exclusive. On Freemasonry's definition that is intolerant - the Moslem, the Hindu, the Jew and all the others cannot and will not accept Jesus as the only way to God. They deny His deity. They deny His sacrifice on Calvary for the sins of the world.

Can you see why there is a serious problem Freemasonry? The Liturgy I quoted from on page 22 went on to state that there was nothing to offend the Moslem, the Hindu or the Jew. If that is the case, then it must offend Christians because the others deny the way of true salvation through Jesus Christ alone.

THE RELIGION OF FREEMASONRY

The Grand Secretary of the Grand Lodge of New Zealand wrote that **"Freemasonry is not a religion although its teachings have a religious character."** He is copying a quote used widely in Masonic literature. This really is double-talk. If you look like a sheep, "baa" like a sheep, live with other sheep and grow wool like other sheep then you shouldn't mind when we call you a sheep. Belief in a Supreme Being is compulsory (except in the Grand Orient), lodge buildings are modelled on temples, hymns are sung, a 'Volume of the Sacred Law' is prominent, (maybe the Bible, or the Koran, the Book of Mormon, the Hindu's Vedas or Upanishads, etc.), there is a Chaplain and an altar, a "Worshipful Master," prayers are offered, there is worship, ritual and the demand for a commitment to the grave along with the offer of salvation to the "Grand Lodge in the sky." It sounds like a religion, but let us carefully check their own authorities before we jump to confusions.

According to W. L. Wilmhurst, "*A brother may legitimately say 'Masonry is my religion.'*"[8] Henry Wilson Coil says that Masonry is a religion as defined by the dictionary, and also fits the definition of a church as well.[9] Dr. Albert Mackey was the High Priest of the General Grand Chapter and Secretary-General of the Southern Supreme Council of 33°. He states "*Freemasonry may rightfully claim to be called a religious institution.*"[10] Frank Higgins wrote that "*Freemasonry is the parent of all religion.*"[11] J. S. M. Ward wrote "*Freemasonry is a significant organised school of mysticism entitled to be called a religion.*"[12] According to Sovereign Grand Commander Albert Pike,

N.Z. Master Mason's Certificate

Why are there so many pagan, occultic and witchcraft symbols used in the membership certificate of the Grand Lodge of New Zealand? (Other certificates are similar.) These include "The Eye of Horus,"(Egyptian pagan deity); the moon and stars known widely as "Diana and Lucifer;" the Astrological signs on the two front pillars (forbidden in the Bible); the dates beginning with "A.L." - Anno Lucis - the Year of Lucifer; and the black and white floor which signifies the dual nature (both good and evil) of their deity.

"Every Masonic Lodge is a temple of religion, and its teachings are instruction in religion."[13] These men were among the highest ranked Freemasons, all in the 33°. None of them seemed embarrassed about calling Freemasonry a religion.

"For every masonic writer who says that Freemasonry is not a religion, there are five masonic writers who claim that it is a pagan religion. While they may disagree as to which pagan religion, they are all agreed that Christianity is wrong and its teachings must not be allowed in the Lodge. If Freemasonry were truly neutral when it came to religion, like the Boy Scouts, A.A. or the YMCA, then why has it allowed Albert Pike to teach his Aryan religion, Manly P. Hall to teach his Mystery Religion, (Lynn) Perkins to teach New Age Religion, etc., If Christianity cannot be openly taught in the lodge, then neither should any other religion. But the fact that pagan religions are being openly taught in the lodge meetings reveals that Pike's anti-Christian bigotry ...has won the day so far as modern Masonry is concerned," wrote Dr. Robert Morey. [14]

The question is not whether Freemasonry is a religion or not, but rather which kind of religion?

THE MASONIC DEITY

According to Martin Wayne, *"A true Mason must forfeit his own religious beliefs in who God is and accept the new god of Masonry."*[15] One of the fabricated secrets of Freemasonry is the imaginary "lost name of God." This is first revealed to a Freemason only when they are admitted to the Holy Royal Arch degree. Before this God is referred as "The Great Architect of the Universe"; the "Grand Geometrician"; or the "Universal  Ruler." Other building terminology is also used. Freemason's deity is named **"Jahbulon."** Jah is claimed to be Yahweh, or Jehovah of the Jews; Bul or Baal is the fertility god of the Canaanites and Syrians; and On or Osiris is the Egyptian god of the underworld. Christians who believe this "deity" is Jesus are being deceived into committing a blasphemous idolatry! The Old Testament records plainly that God's severest judgement fell on Israel when they worshipped Baal, the evil demonic power who required human sacrifices and other abominations. *(See the story of Elijah in 1 Kings 18.)*

I agree with former Lodge Master Edmond Ronayne, who states *"The very religious philosophy and false worship which caused Jehovah to destroy His own temple and banish into captivity His ancient people, are precisely the same philosophy and worship which modern Masons profess shall fit them for the glories of heaven."*[16]

In some degrees, the deity of Freemasonry is named as **"Abaddon,"** which the Bible describes as a destructive evil spirit (Revelation 9:11). The gods to be worshipped as revealed in the 24° are Osiris, Isis and Horus, from ancient Egypt. In the 26° the gods to be worshipped are Odin, Frea and Thor, from the Druids. In the 31° the ceremony explains ancient Egyptian beliefs regarding the Afterlife, including being taken to the Council of (Egyptian) gods for judgement. In the 32° Scottish Rite it is explained that the Masonic trinity is called **"AUM,"** - A for Brahma the creator; U for Vishnu the preserver; and M for Shiva the destroyer - Hindu deities. (The original letters were in Sanskrit.) **What are all these pagan gods doing in an organisation which claims to be acceptable to Christians?**

One of the major mysteries Freemasons are taught to seek after is enlightenment about the name of the Great Unknowable Deity. The God of the Bible reveals a great deal about Himself through that book, including His name and many of His attributes of personality. **Freemasons are seeking what and who Christians already know.** The One True God of the Bible (see Deuteronomy 6:4 and John 17:3) is not amalgamated with or manifested through these other false deities because they are idolatrous and under God's divine judgement. **"Great is the LORD and most worthy of praise; He is to be feared above all gods. For all the gods of the nations are idols, but the LORD made the heavens."** (1 Chronicles 16:25-26.) **"This is what the LORD says... "I am the first and I am the last; apart from me there is no God."** (Isaiah 44:6). Only Satan himself could be happy at how many men he has deceived through the worship of Freemasonry's false gods.

FALSE PRIESTHOOD, BAPTISM, & COMMUNION

When a Freemason is initiated into the 19° of the A & A/Scottish Rite he is anointed with oil and proclaimed to be a "Priest forever after the Order of Melchizedek." Hebrews 7:24 states that this Order of Melchizedek is unchangeable (Strongs 531 = *"aparabatos"* in the Greek, the exclusive and untransferable) possession of Jesus Christ. It cannot be shared with anyone else, and the term can also mean *"without successor."* This means that any person who claims to belong to this order, according to the Bible, is claiming to be Jesus Christ. The credentials to be Israel's Messiah and the Saviour of the World are required from all who have passed through the 19°. Otherwise they are guilty of a great blasphemy. The same applies to all Mormon men who enter their Melchizedek Priesthood.

In the 26° the Candidate is baptised in water "*for his soul's purification.*" It is then free, following death, to return to the Universal Soul or deity. This is blatant Gnosticism, has much in common with Buddhism, and is a blasphemy to Christians, as well as to Jews and Moslems.

The 18° is often held up as the "Christian Degree," but reading through the ceremony shows there is a warping of the Scriptures which disproves this claim. The symbols used include the Pelican (which feeds its young with its own blood - a mockery of Communion); the blood red Rose (which is claimed to be the symbol of secrecy and silence, and also the symbol of dawn - the resurrection of light); and the serpent (the mythical symbol of wisdom). This 18° ceremony claims that the death of Jesus was a "dire calamity." Why? Surely only those who reject the atoning work of Jesus Christ on the Cross of Calvary could suggest such a thing. If this were truly a "Christian degree" as is claimed, the death and resurrection of Jesus Christ should be boldly proclaimed as the ultimate victory over sin and evil. Wrongly claiming the work at Calvary as a calamity again proves both the anti-Christian bias of Freemasonry, and that individual Freemasons have not understood the Bible message of Christ's atoning work.

THE MYTHS OF HIRAM ABIFF

In the ritual of the Third or Master Mason Degree there is acted out the myth of Hiram Abiff. Every Fellowcraft Freemason being initiated into the Third degree represents Hiram Abiff, and the mythical drama unfolds in such a convincing way it is usually accepted as historic fact. Most of this story, however, is a fabrication to suit the pagan rituals and purposes of Freemasonry. For example, nowhere in the Bible is there any mention of his death.

Hiram is portrayed as a senior workman in brass and other metals during the construction of Israel's temple in Jerusalem during the time of King Solomon. Three Fellowcraft or 2nd Degree men demand to learn from Hiram the secret of the Master Mason. These men shake and push Hiram around, and when he refuses to divulge the secret, he is killed by the third ruffian. His body is then hastily buried to cover the crime. After being missed, a search locates Hiram's body buried under an Acacia tree. While others of lower rank vainly attempt to resurrect Hiram, the Worshipful Master, representing King Solomon, then raises him from the dead, given through the Five Points of Fellowship, and then gives him eternal life.

It should be pointed out that Hiram allegedly came from Phoenicia, a country which worshipped the pagan deity Baal, the Sun god. History and the Bible records that King Solomon fell into idolatry through his acceptance of this and other pagan gods. While using Bible characters and some verses to tell this story, most is myth concocted during the past two centuries.

According to the Masonic version of events, Hiram's body is later reburied near the temple. This is not a resurrection but a reinterment. Resurrected people aren't reburied! But the mythical symbolism of Hiram's raising does have a purpose. According to eminent Masonic scholar Albert Mackey, "...*the succeeding portions of the legend are intended to convey the sublime symbolism of a resurrection from the grave, and a new birth into a future life.*" [29]

Mackey goes on to describe the Masonic hope of each member, after yielding to death, being then raised into eternity by a word from the "Grand Master of the Universe", followed by drawing near the divine presence. Only one possible conclusion can be drawn from this - immortality is offered through the legend of Hiram Abiff. Many Masonic scholars, including Mackey, Carl Claudy, Joseph Fort Newton as well as many Ritual books/Monitors all agree on this.

When a man has been through the ritual described above, his attention is drawn to the only light in the lodge, (all other lights are out) which is above the Master's chair on the eastern side of the lodge. It is called the "Star in the East." The Initiate is then told *"The light of a Master Mason is Darkness Visible."* Since Satan/Lucifer is described as the Prince of Darkness, the reference can only mean one thing - Lucifer receives his due worship here. If this was meant to imply Jesus Christ, then why not say so? Jesus said, **"I am the Light of the World. He who follows Me shall not walk in darkness, but have the light of life,"** (John 8:12). Jesus never did anything in darkness. The Star in the East alludes to the "Wise Men" who came from the East to find the baby Jesus in the manger. (Maybe someone should provide a compass here, because the wise men came *from* the East, and *went* West to find Jesus who is the Truth, according to John 14:6.)

A skull and crossbones (or sometimes a whole skeleton) are shown by torch to the Initiate at this time. Several former Freemasons have confirmed these are real bones, not plastic models. Isn't there a law against having human body parts in one's possession unless you are involved in medical research? Morality strongly suggests we shouldn't be playing around with someone's remains. Enough people have been converted out of Witchcraft where similar rituals are observed to suggest this is an evil practise, about which there is nothing good.

Hiram Abiff brings the wrong message to Freemasons, and again confirms both the mythology taught as fact, and the false offer of immortality offered by Freemasonry and rejected by Jesus Christ.

IS FREEMASONRY RECYCLED PAGANISM?

Many authorities, both Freemasons and others, have stated that Freemasonry is just the religious beliefs of Paganism. Paganism has been defined as "the occult worship of Nature, attributing to gods and goddesses aspects of nature." This is primarily understood to be a revival of the ancient Egyptian, Greek and Babylonian mystery religions. Here are some quotes which illustrate this.

"In the Blue Degrees an initiate is initiated into the Egyptian Trinity of the ancient mysteries of Egypt. And this Egyptian Trinity is hidden from the initiate. He does not know at all what he is being initiated into..."[17] (British author, researcher and cult expert, Ian Taylor.)

"The God of nineteen-twentieths of the Christian world is only Bel, Moloch, Zeus, or at best Osiris, Mithras, or Adonai, under another name, worshipped with the old Pagan ceremonies and ritualistic formulas. It is the Statue of Olympian Jove, worshipped as the Father, in the Christian Church that was a pagan temple; It is the Statue of Venus, become the Virgin Mary."[18] (Albert Pike, 33°.)

"The religious cults in the Graeco-Roman world, Egypt, Greece, Rome, etc., were known as the Ancient Mysteries. These powerful fraternities had very many things in common with our own craft."[19] (M. Haywood, Founder of Masonic Study Club.)

"There is a certain difference between... the Christian religion, and the old Egyptian mystery-faith from which Masonry is derived." [20] (Bishop C.W. Leadbeater, 33°.)

"The Worshipful Master represents the Rising Sun."[21] (J.S.M. Ward.) Every Master Mason knows this.

"The point within a circle is derived from sun worship, and is, in reality, of phallic origin. It is the symbol of the universe, the sun being represented by the point, while the circumference is the universe."[22] (Past Grand Master Dr. Albert Mackey, 33°.)

"Bacchus died and rose again on the golden Asian plain,
Osiris rose from out the grave and thereby mankind did save,
Adonis likewise shed his blood by the yellow Syrian flood,
Zoroaster brought to birth Mithra from His Cave of Earth;
And today in Christian Lands We with them can join hands."[23]

(J.S.M. Ward.)

"Lucifer, the Light-Bearer! Lucifer, the Son of the Morning! Strange and mysterious name to give to the Spirit of Darkness! Is it he who bears the Light, and with its splendours intolerable blinds feeble, sensual or selfish Souls? Doubt it not." [24] (Albert Pike.)

"It is admitted that the secret system of Freemasonry was originally founded on the Mysteries of the Egyptian Isis, the goddess-mother, or wife of Osiris." [25] (Alexander Hislop.)

The above are an interesting range of authoritative comments, mostly by senior Freemasons. Obviously there are many other quotes I could mention, but space prevents that. So, are Freemasons Satanists? Not at all. Whether the members know it or not, the god of Freemasonry is Lucifer. Are there any differences between Satan and Lucifer? Yes; Luciferians imagine they are doing good, while Satanists know they are evil. The Bible describes Lucifer as the most important angel God created. When he rebelled against God, Lucifer was thrown out of heaven along with the angels who joined the first ever attempted revolution. From that day of eviction Lucifer was known as Satan. *"The real secret of all the secret societies is that they believe Lucifer never fell to earth; that Lucifer is God, and has been since the dawn of creation,"*[26] wrote author William Still.

Luciferians believe God has a dual nature. They claim he is the good god Lucifer, and the bad god Adonai, both equal in power yet opposite in intent. This is sometimes represented by the circular Yin/Yang symbol of the Taoists and Buddhists, or the black and white checkerboard pattern with the tessellated boarders found in Masonic buildings, (See *the floor shown on* *page 26).* Lucifer is sometimes further divided into Isis (the female principal), and Osiris (the male principal). The core myth at the centre of all secret societies is that Lucifer is benevolent, seeking to illuminate his followers with special knowledge.

Lucifer became Satan when he fell, and his benevolence fell with him. Even Satanists know that Lucifer is one of Satan's myths, aimed at deceiving mankind with false promises of power, wisdom and knowledge. Freemasonry is not spiritually benign just because men in its highest degrees admit they worship Lucifer.

The Western calendar numbers years from the alleged birth year of Jesus Christ. B.C. equals 'Before Christ,' while A.D. means 'Anno Domini,' - the "Year of the Lord." (More recent evidence confirms Jesus was born in either 3 or 4 B.C.) The Masonic calendar marks years by A.L., meaning 'Anno Lucis,' the 'Year of Light" or the 'Year of Lucifer.' Both are correct.

Since Freemasons teach that the death of Jesus Christ was a tragedy, they don't count their years like the rest of society. This is played out in the ceremonies of the 18°, (the Rose Croix, or Rosicrucian degree). The reason given by their authorities is that the day Jesus was crucified was the birth of Christianity, ever to be the antagonist of Freemasonry, according to their historian Abbe Augusten de Barruel.

It may be true to describe Freemasonry as "Recycled Paganism." However, the spiritual explanation is that a group of people, mostly men, have allowed themselves to be deceived by the arch-deceiver, Satan, whose primary interest is to draw people's worship from the True God to himself. If you want to back the winner of this contest, then read to the end of the Bible, where God has Satan/Lucifer put into a burning pit where he will remain for eternity (Revelation 20:10). God does not want any one of His creatures, including you, to join Satan. That is why He sent Jesus to pay for the penalty for your sins. Those who reject God's offer of salvation will learn the hard way they made a mistake, with eternal consequences. Let us look at three last quotes.

"It is impossible to exaggerate the difference between the god of Masonry and the God of the Christian. The two conceptions are poles asunder. The difference is so vital that no intelligent Christian can possibly overlook it..." [27] (Dr. C.N. Button, endorsed by the Grand Master of Victoria, Australia.)

"If it is wrong for a Christian to pray together with a Jew or a Moslem (or any member of another religion) to the Great Architect, then it is undoubtedly wrong for him to become a Mason..." [28] (Vindex, Masonic apologist.) He is right - it is wrong!

"Do not be yoked together with unbelievers. For what do righteousness and wickedness have in common? Or what fellowship can light have with darkness? What harmony is there between Christ and Belial? *(The system of Satanic worship).* **What does a believer have in common with an unbeliever? What agreement is there between the temple of God and idols?... Therefore come out from them and be separate, says the Lord."** (2 Corinthians, 6:14-17).

Prince Rose Croix Certificate

TERRARUM ORBIS ARCHITECTONIS AD GLORIAM UNIVERSI INGENTIS

ORDO AB CHAO

Supreme Council of the XXXIII. Degree

OF THE

ANCIENT AND ACCEPTED RITE OF H.R.D.M. K·H.

From the East of the Supreme Council of the Sovereign Grand Inspectors General of the 33° of the ANCIENT AND ACCEPTED RITE for England and Wales and its Districts and Chapters Overseas, under the C.C. of the Zenith, near the B.B., answering to N.L. 51° 31', Long. 6' W.M. of Greenwich.

O all Very Illustrious Sovereign Grand Inspectors General ; Most Valiant and Sublime Princes of the Royal Secret ; Grand Inspectors Inquisitor Commander ; Grand Elected Knights K∴, H∴ ; Excellent and Perfect Princes Rose Croix; Grand, Ineffable, Sublime, Free and Accepted Masons of every Degree of Masonry throughout the Universe, and

To all to whom These Presents may come

LIGHT, LIFE, LOVE.

Know ye, That We, the Supreme Council of the 33° for England and Wales and its Districts and Chapters Overseas, do hereby certify, acknowledge and proclaim our Excellent Brother,

to be an Expert Master of the Symbolic Lodges; Secret Master; Perfect Master; Intimate Secretary; Provost and Judge; Intendant of the Buildings; Elect of Nine; Elect of Fifteen; Sublime Elect; Grand Master Architect; Ancient Master of the Royal Arch of Enoch; Grand Elect Perfect and Sublime Master.

And do also Certify: That at the _____ Chapter Rose Croix
of H.R.D.M. No. _____ held at _____ NEW ZEALAND _____
on the _____ day of _____ the said Brother having been duly installed Knight
of the Sword, or of the East, Prince of Jerusalem, and Knight of the East and West, was received
admitted and constituted, an

EXCELLENT AND PERFECT PRINCE ROSE CROIX OF H.R.D.M., 18°

In Testimony whereof, the Grand Secretary General has hereunto subscribed his
name and affixed the Seals in the Grand Council Chamber at London this _____ day
of the month of _____ A.L. 5 9 8 6 , A.D. 1 9 8 6 .

—33°

Grand Secretary General H∴E∴.

WHO OPPOSES FREEMASONRY?

I have presented much evidence explaining why a true Christian could not be a Freemason. This view is shared widely, including by John and Charles Wesley, General William Booth, D. L. Moody, Dr. R. A. Torrey, Charles Finney and a host of other prominent Christian leaders over several centuries, all of whom condemned Masonry. They are not alone. Let me run quickly through a list of Christian denominations which oppose Masonry. The World bodies of The Salvation Army, Greek Orthodox, Lutheran, Methodist, Presbyterian, Mennonite, Nazarene, Churches of Christ and Pentecostal churches, Brethren Assemblies, The Church of England, The Free Church of Scotland, British Methodists, and the Baptist Union of Scotland, whose report has been endorsed and published by New Zealand, British and Irish Baptist Unions. In June 1993 the Southern Baptists of America agreed that Freemasonry is pagan, unscriptural and in conflict with basic Christian beliefs. Despite this, they still compromised their report, probably for fear of loss of revenue from Freemasons who might resign or stop giving. Such manipulative tactics have been used quite often and only confirm that such men cannot be walking with Jesus Christ. Some Freemasons hold positions of control in some denominations, so discussion on this vexed issue has been avoided or stifled.

In addition to the above, virtually every Pope of the Roman Catholic Church between 1738 and 1981 has required instant excommunication for any Catholic who becomes a Freemason. Author David Yallop claimed there were seventeen Freemasons on the Vatican Council. I won't attempt to explain this, but it has been confirmed by former 33° Freemason and Grand Chaplain of New York, Rev. Harmon Taylor. Now when you tally that list up there are few which compromise over this issue. I can find no evidence of any Christian denomination which supports Freemasonry. In spite of such overwhelming opposition from Christians, there are still some Lodges who persist in proclaiming that Christianity continues to provide the foundation of Freemasonry. The evidence says otherwise.

CONTROLLING THE PULPIT AND THE CHURCH

Most Christian pastors know there is a problem if Freemasonry is present in their congregation. Having asked widely, I can report there is no evidence that Freemasons are actively involved in Christian evangelism in local churches or elsewhere. If they are involved in their local church, they will usually get into the finance and/or administration areas, to control what happens in the church.

Many pastors are afraid to preach a message which is critical of the teachings and practices of Freemasonry. However, once a pastor knows that Freemasonry is incompatible with the Christian faith, if he or she still won't address this in their church, their ministry has become compromised and they will become accountable to God for the blood of others, as recorded in Ezekiel. **"But if the watchman see the sword come, and blow not the trumpet, and the people be not warned; if the sword come, and take any person from among them, he is taken away in his iniquity; but his blood will I require at the watchman's hands"** (Ezekiel 33:6). Since Christian pastors are intended by God to fulfil the role of "watchmen", looking after the spiritual and other welfare of their congregation, they are more responsible. (There are also many non-Christian pastors in pulpits, who aren't born again and in relationship with Jesus Christ, and they cannot lead their people above their own level of spiritual maturity, which is really heathenism).

Having said that, when a Christian pastor does take a stand against this false religion hiding in their church, in all probability they will end up with a fight on their hands. I have seen this occur a number of times. There is often division, church splits, confusion, hurting people, especially among the older age group who have been kept in ignorance of the true nature of Freemasonry by relatives who were involved in a lodge. "But they were good men" goes the common cry of such folks. The evidence is beginning to show just the opposite. I was approached by the pastor and eldership of an Evangelical church to come and present a teaching on Freemasonry. They had heard me speak somewhere else, and observed the fruit of changed lives. They wanted to get on proclaiming the Gospel of Jesus Christ. There was no other agenda: they wanted to see people saved, baptised, discipled and going on for Jesus Christ. They did have a dozen families in their church with significant Freemasonry connections, who were acting in concert to seek to control this congregation. The leadership had correctly discerned that Freemasonry had acted as a giant smothering blanket over the outreach of this congregation. (This has been reported to me by evangelists and others on every continent and in many countries, so isn't a new discovery or an invented one.) The Freemasonry families were content with a "spiritual" social club rather than a vibrant expression of Christ at work on earth through His body.

I had warned the pastor and elders they would be in for a spiritual and emotional rodeo once they commenced. The leadership discussed and affirmed inviting me to speak at a date some six months out, and also drafted a formal statement on the incompatibility of Freemasonry with the Christian/Biblical foundations of their denomination. Within days, the Freemasons in that congregation tried to call a congregational meeting to have the pastor removed over some invented trifle. Most of the people saw through this ruse and didn't support it. The Freemasons then went to the state executive of their denomination to have the credentials of the pastor revoked. Since he had been a faithful and fruitful pastor in previous congregations prior to coming to this one, his past record prevented any such action. The denominational executive appreciated the pastor's integrity, but not that of the Freemasons.

The true spiritual power and agenda behind Freemasonry was revealed through the various attempts to control this congregation. These included control, manipulation, division, confusion, dishonesty and a care for bricks and mortar rather than people. By the time I arrived to teach, there was almost shell-shock among the congregation. Permanent damage was only prevented by genuine and caring pastoring by the leadership. After I had completed my teaching session (which had standing room only), several men came up to me and thanked me for the accuracy of my material, and confessed they had been former Freemasons themselves. Not a single current Freemason or their family members attended that meeting, which shows a certain bigotry. Now that the congregation had the facts about Freemasonry, and had seen first hand the spiritual blindness of Lodge members, they adopted the leadership's statement, including banning any leader from belonging to any such organisation. All dozen Freemason families left that church and went to infest another church in town.

There are some in ministry who might not want to endure such a difficult time in order the deal with Freemasonry in their church. I would ask if your congregation are worth fighting for? I had asked for prayer from our own intercessors for this congregation. I know they also had their own, and several other local churches of various denominations upheld them in prayer during this time. I contacted the pastor again several times, including once some six months later. This was to find out the fruit of the work. The pastor told me that salvations had been significant, and in fact more had been saved during the past six months than the previous five years, and baptisms were the same. Despite a temporary dip in income from tithes and offerings with the departure of the Freemasons and their families, the pastor informed me they were now ahead of budget and were able to plan major outreachs with other local churches to reach their community with the Gospel of Jesus Christ. Despite the difficulties they went through, the faithfulness of God cannot be understated. True pastors will want to protect their congregation from the effects of Freemasonry and other deceptions.

HERESIES WITHIN FREEMASONRY

This list was complied by clergy looking into Freemasonry for the report of the General Synod of the Church of England in 1988.

Syncretism. This claims different religions are equally valid, or may be treated as equal or fused together. Dangerous compromises are committed in a vain attempt to reconcile differing belief systems or understanding of God which are incompatible.

Dualism. Masonic and Christian perceptions of God are in serious conflict. No Christian could subscribe to both without suffering spiritual schizophrenia.

Polytheism. While a Freemason on his own may believe in only one God (even the one true God) he must welcome all fellow Freemason's gods at Masonry's altar.

Socinianism. Masons elevate God the Father at the expense of God the Son.

Pelagianism. This claims that man was not cursed with original sin, but may achieve perfection on earth and heaven through good works, rather then by faith in Jesus Christ and what He accomplished at Calvary. Christians believe all have sinned and can only be redeemed through repentance of sin and trusting in Christ and what He did.

Rationalism. Freemasonry's titles of Great Architect and Great Geometrician imply God merely built this world and does not intervene in its affairs. Christians know that God asserts Hid will and purposes through His Son, Jesus Christ, and through the Holy Spirit.

Gnosticism. Salvation is falsely claimed to be obtainable through learning secret knowledge, a view explicitly rejected by many New Testament writers and all Christians. Also, salvation is such good news is must be shared. Any salvation kept secret from others is not a true salvation but the penalty of deception.

Manicheanism. God isn't all good but the source of both good and evil.

Idolatry. Several parts of Masonic ritual break the second commandment by having graven images and bowing to them in worship.

Satanism. All worship not directed solely to the One True God must be, by reason, directed at the arch-enemy, Satan.

A former Knight's Templar confirmed to me that Freemasonry's Blue Lodge Ritual requires a man to break 5 of the Ten Commandments, number's 1, 2, 3, 6, and 9; quite apart from any others broken elsewhere in one's life. I will believe Freemasonry is Christian *only when* every Lodge Chaplain calls for every member present to repent of their sins and put their faith and trust in the Lord Jesus Christ alone for their eternal salvation. Until that happens, the evidence is overwhelming that Freemasonry is a pagan religious organisation whose members are among the most self-righteous in the religious world.

As I was completing revision of this book, I came across the following relevant quotation. *"What then is a false religion? Since God is holy and man is sinful, we define a false religion as a religion that has not settled the sin question; a religion that has not taken lying, idolatry, pride, adultery, anger, and all forms of wickedness from a man and yet promises that same man some euphoria here or in heaven. That is what should be considered a false religion. Who then is a worshipper of a false god? He is the one who worships an idol. If an idol is a false representation of God or a god, and the worshipper has never seen such a being in reality, it means that an idol is a false god. A doll, no matter how fine, is a false child, and a mannequin a false man. Apart from physical images, if a man conceives of God as different from the one only true God of the Bible and worships such a 'God', no matter how sincere he may be, he is just like the one who has made a physical image to represent God. Any 'God' that emerges out of such imagination is a false god. Our knowledge of God is from revelation and not imagination. A.W. Tozer says, "Do not try to imagine God or you will have an imaginary God.""* [29]

THE FRUITS OF FREEMASONRY - A SUMMARY

Fruit	Explanation	Scriptures show God forbids
Pride	Titles egotistical, pretending to be aristocracy or military of middle ages. inflated with self-importance BUT: we are called to be servants, humble	Matt. 20:25-28, 1 Tim 3:6, Pro 16:18 Matt 11:29, Phil. 2:3 Isaiah 14:13-15, James 4:6
Self-Righteousness	A member's proven character & good standing in community required prior to joining. Brings vain sense of being good enough (by works) to stand before God without a Saviour.	John 5:38-40 2 Corint. 3:5-6 Luke 18:9-14 Matt. 15:4-11
Idolatry	Local lodge leader called "Worshipful Master", "GAOTU" is not God of Bible BUT: worship God alone, & call no man "master"	Matt 22:36-38 Exodus 20:2-4
Unequally Yoked	Members required to believe in a supreme being, not God of Bible. Brothers join at altar of pagans praying to false gods	2 Cor 6:14-18, Ex. 34:11-16 1 Cor. 10:20-22, 2 John 9
Deliberate Deceit Dishonesty & Corruption	Leaders admit deliberate deceit over Blue Lodge members, despite ritual teaching morality. Ritual instructs preference to a fellow mason in business & society, regardless of merit	Titus 1:10-11 2 Cor. 4:2
False Concept of God	FM claims God is source of good & evil also that Jesus & Lucifer are 2 sides of same deity. Represented in black & white flooring	2 Cor. 5:21, 1 Sam. 2:2 John 14:30, 1 John 1:5 Isaiah 6:3
Secrecy	Shown in much ritual, passwords, handshakes, etc. Many trivial, some embarrassing	John 18:20, Mark 4:22

Swearing Oaths	Oaths & obligations given 1 phrase at time, with a penalty invoking a curse, then ask God to witness what He forbids.	Matt 5:33-37, James 5:12 Exodus 20:7, Lev. 5:4-5
Greed	Many/most Masons join hope for business social or financial promotion, despite denial	Titus 1:11, 1 Tim. 3:3-8 1 Peter 5:2
False Assurance of salvation	All Masons, regardless of beliefs, are offered immortality & heaven in Blue Lodge Ritual	Rom. 10:9, John 3:16,18,19 Luke 7:47-48
False Resurrection	Ritual of 3^0 - Master Mason involves the ceremonial killing & resurrection of candidate	Hebrews 9:27, Romans 10:9 Romans 3:10-12
Anger & Violence	The violence and ceremonial killing of the Master Mason brings fruit of anger, noticed in most Masons.	Proverbs 14:7, Eph. 4:26, 31
Spiritual Blindness & Searching	Every holy book is "on the Level" during ceremonies, resulting in belief that all religions are part of the true religion. Children & grand children of Masons often get into cults & strange religions or beliefs due to this inherited influence, because any god will do. The blindness is caused by the spirit invited in with the hoodwink.	Galatians 1:8-9,
Fear	Enters with the sudden noises while blindfolded; & with spear. compass etc. pressed into naked left breast during 1st degree initiation	2 Timothy 1:7; Hebrews 13:6 1 Peter 2:17; 1 John 4:18
Curses	Arise from all the above. A curse without cause cannot alight, but these issues are the causes, so are justified by Scripture. Good News! The effects can be removed when the causes are renounced and repented of.	Galatians 1:8-9, Proverbs 26:2

TESTIMONY OF "ALAN,"
former 30° Mason and retired Anglican lawyer

"I still have many friends in Masonry that I look upon with affection and respect. Many of them are decent and well-intentioned people who I believe went into Masonry for the same reason I did, in that they understood it was a Christian-based organisation, in that it gave a humanitarian lifestyle, good fellowship and promoted a moral standard of life. Masonry is like quite a lot of other things, in that it has sufficient moral teaching in it, and even verses taken from the Bible, to give a false sense of security as to what it is.

My disagreement is not with all those individual people who are in the Craft, but with the hidden agenda that lies in Masonry with indoctrination, with false interpretations and a deliberate deceit, particularly the majority of Masons who are in the Blue Lodge. I was one who went right through to the thirtieth degree. I have come to a realisation that it is <u>only when you reach the upper degrees of Masonry that the true significance of Masonic teachings are made apparent</u> in any way. It was following my commitment to Christ with the Baptism of the Holy Spirit that I knew I had committed a very great wrong, and that it had to be put right. I admit frankly that there were selfish reasons for my going into Masonry. During the war years when I was overseas I was curious about the fact that some of the men in the unit every now and then went off into a little hush-hush gathering somewhere, and to any enquiries I made they said "We've got a lodge meeting." I didn't know anything more about it than that. I came back from the war and went into my family law practice, married shortly afterwards to my very precious wife and within just over six years we had six children. That sounds pretty hot going, but we had two sets of twins on end, so there wasn't time for much else, and I forgot my curiosity about Masonry for most of that time. I had a business associate who was also a relative of mine by marriage, and who had been a senior officer in the unit I served with. He kept speaking to me about the advantages to be gained from joining Masonry. He knew we were active members of a church, and claimed Masonry was a Christian-based organisation. I expressed some interest in it, and was eventually invited to join the lodge.

I am blessed with a fairly retentive memory and my progress up the ladder in Masonry was rapid for that reason. I soon went through the first three degrees and then the various offices in the lodge. I finished up as "Worshipful Master," and then at a later stage (I suppose in recognition of my known Christian commitment) I was invited to join the Rose Croix degree, the 18th degree. Much later on I was invited into the 30th degree. Even through that period of time there were a number of things which continued to cause some unease within me in some way or other, and I didn't know quite how to deal with them, but I want to share some of those with you. They steadily grew until finally I knew I had to leave the lodge completely, after about 30 years in it.

The first of these items which caused me concern was <u>the issue of secrecy</u>, because I wondered, if the teachings of Masonry were so true and good, why was it necessary to keep them hidden in a veil of secrecy. I couldn't even share those concerns with my wife, close friends or my spiritual leaders, and had to have that blanket of silence over the things that were revealed to me in Masonry. I talked with my wife afterwards about her feelings and she disclosed to me that when I went in she first of all felt bewilderment, then resentment, and finally reluctant acceptance. I am just so grateful that our marriage wasn't endangered, but she was helped over those years by a good group of lodge wives, many of whom had the same feelings, and they were able to share together.

The next thing which worried me was the question of Masonic oaths. I now recognise them as blood oaths, but even without that recognition if you just look at them word by word, they are horrendous. They agree to a vile mutilation of the body in different ways as a penalty for revealing the secrets, before those secrets are even disclosed to the Initiate. This applies to every step in Masonry. You have to agree to accept the teachings before knowing what they are.

The next point I had problems with right through was the question of deception and double meanings and euphemisms used in the rituals, particularly in the first three degrees. The definition of Masonry itself given to members gives some sort of clue of this, that it is "a peculiar system of morals, veiled in allegory and illustrated by symbols." That certainly gives some hint of what is involved. I was told it was a Christian-based organisation, and I knew quite a number of churchmen who were in the Craft, and I thought if it was okay for them then it must be okay for me. But I have realised, after thinking it over carefully, that God is never called God, but the "Great Architect of the Universe," and finally the passwords and signs which were exchanged in a secret way, but never had the meanings been given. These were a few of the matters which gave me unease at that stage. Even in the 18th Rose Croix degree, which is supposed to be the Christian form of Masonry, I came to see there were some parts of the ritual which had a secret hidden connotation with elements of the occult there.

The final problem I had was the matter of obedience to the Master and the governing authorities of the craft. The Master takes a significant part in the Craft Degree rituals. He leads the Initiate from "darkness to light" with a sharp instrument pressed against his breast. He leads the Fellow Craft from "death to resurrection" and one can't but wonder if this is a symbolic usurping of the place of Christ in our Christian teachings, putting Masonic teachings at total variance with the Word of God.

There are quite a lot of other things which I came to question, but perhaps I will summarise at this point. I came out of Masonry about ten years ago, because in the meantime we had together increased our Christian commitment considerably. The first real questioning of Masonry came through a very close friend of ours who was a retired clergyman, and who was Spirit-filled (filled with God's Holy Spirit). He had had family members who were involved in Masonry and felt a very deep concern about it. Through him we were both baptised in the Holy Spirit and from then on my move away from Masonry increased rapidly. You couldn't worship and live in the Holy Spirit and remain with those areas of concern. When I finally left I felt a tremendous release and freedom, and the joy that we have shared together in these retirement years and the blessings in healing and restoration of relationships and provision from our loving and caring God are more than adequate answers to the decision I made.

TESTIMONY OF "HAVELL"
former Master Mason

"For eight years I was a Freemason, initiated, passed, and raised, if you know the jargon. It simply means I was in the Blue Lodge, and I became in due course a Master Mason. I was introduced into Freemasonry by two members of a church vestry of which I was also a member. I liked and respected both men - they were friends, and I had no reason to doubt their honesty. They would say, in accord with Freemasonry teachings, that I was not invited to join, but rather that I expressed an interest. That is one of the things which is part of Freemasonry folklore; that no one is invited to join, that a candidate expresses an interest and it is that interest that is subsequently taken up. So two respected friends said this was something I should look at, I expressed an interest and some two years later I was initiated into a lodge.

However, nine years ago I decided to resign from my lodge. Then I removed all lodge-related clothing and books from my home, and finally I renounced entirely all connections with Freemasonry and sought the LORD's forgiveness. Why did I choose to do that? Well, let me start with some of the good things, the attractive things about Freemasonry, and perhaps you will come on a journey with me as I work through the list to some of the things I am uncomfortable with about Freemasonry.

Freemasons are known for, but generally don't seek publicity for, good works. For example, the building of homes for the elderly, and support for widows and children. Many Freemasons give a great deal of time and considerable sums of money to that sort of thing. Lodge ritual promotes high standards of moral conduct, for example, honesty, uprightness, support for widows and children. They acknowledge a supreme being, any supreme being. For the Christian or Jew it is Yahweh, but for Moslems it is Allah, for others, their gods.

It is quite spurious to hold that all are the same, the one true God. Neither the Christian nor the Jew may have any God other than the Lord God the creator. That is the first commandment, and to the Christian, God has uniquely revealed Himself in Jesus Christ. To acknowledge any other god is not only to reject the First Commandment, but also to deny Christ. Christ said, "*If you deny me I also shall deny you before My Father in heaven.*" So I believe that Freemasons, on this alone, are in grave spiritual danger. Perhaps one could express it more strongly than this.

Next, Paul instructed Christians not to be yoked together with unbelievers. In my view candidates undertaking the first three degrees of Freemasonry yoke themselves with members of other lodges who may openly acknowledge supreme beings other than God. Much lodge ritual calls on Freemasons to do good works, so that they may ascend to heaven. In contrast Christ said that no man comes to the Father except through Him. He is the way. Paul makes clear that we cannot justify ourselves through good works. Only our faith in Christ is cause for hope, that we will share eternal life with Him. To argue otherwise is again to deny Christ.

Continuing on with falsehood, Freemasonry claims that lodge ritual is largely a series of plays that teach morality. Well, certainly they are fiction. The plays, however, present as fact what is fiction, so they may be plays but they have the presentation of being truth. But in the course of this, Bible stories are mistold and Biblical characters are given roles that they don't ever have in the Bible. There is no biblical support for it. Now, I think Freemasons might argue that this is but a means, albeit an amoral or immoral means, to an end. But I view it as an insidious form of lie. It is falsehood with a religious gloss, and for traditional Anglicans the gloss is also enhanced by a wording which is a counterfeit of 1662 Prayer Book language. So it has this religiosity about it which appeals to people who know that tradition, which affects for example, many Presbyterians and Anglicans.

Now Freemasons learn their lodge ritual by heart. "By heart" is a significant phrase. By repeated listening to the ritual and reciting it, members become skilful at presenting it from memory. And this aggravates the danger. Much of what you learn you internalise. But it is not truth, it is falsehood. It is certainly not God's truth. Can I ask you, who wants us to be skilful in presenting falsehood? This same sort of rote learning and reiteration are used by evil regimes seeking to perpetuate themselves. So we put the same mechanism and manipulation to work.

Lodge ritual is agreed among Freemasons to be secret. The fact is, of course, that the ritual is largely available through books in most public libraries. However, as you proceed from one degree to another there are always new "secrets" to be learned, and most of us only get into the Blue Lodge and don't see beyond that. However, the problem is that the meaning of this ritual is obscure and questionable. In my judgement, there is sufficient evidence of hidden evil in the lodge ritual to repel any Christian.

It came to a point where I could no longer accept this accumulation of evil. It stood against everything I believed about the Lord and everything I had come to understand about the way He works. So I got out. It took me a long time before I got rid of my lodge regalia and books. I put them out in the garage, and then finally I had them burnt by a friend. It was reported to us by this friend, a priest, that when he had burnt it, there was nothing left. The metal buckles, the hinges, there was nothing - it had gone completely. That day my wife and I found a new freedom, and I rejoice for it. "

(The above testimonies were both delivered in public meetings. Minor grammatical and other editing has been necessary to convert what they said to writing. The spirit of their messages remains unchanged.)

TESTIMONY OF "SCOTT"

"While I have never been in the Masons and always held them off at arm's length, most of the men in my mother's and father's families were heavily involved. At the suggestion of my pastor I came to your site to use your Prayer of Release from the Freemasons. I didn't have any illnesses, but have suffered from a sort of mild, chronic depression which seems to have been passed down through my father's family.

My wife and I prayed the Prayer of Freedom from Religious Spirits first (on Jubilee's website) and then came back last night for the Masons Prayer. To be honest, it's a long prayer and I thought it would be a waste of time, since I've never taken any Masonic oaths nor been involved in their rites.

Was I wrong! As soon as we began reading the prayer the Holy Spirit began to move powerfully, and my wife received a vision of the room filling with angels. The energy in the room was palpable, and felt by everyone present, including my two sons, aged 13 and 11.

I don't know exactly what was broken last night, nor how it was related to Masonry, but we know that spiritual warfare occurred, chains were broken and we were released from something evil that had attached itself to us through my father's and his ancestors' submission to the Masons.

I would never have thought what they did in the past could have an effect on my family and me today, but I am convinced now.

Thank you for publishing these prayers on your website and allowing their use by anyone who needs them."

REMOVING THE HOODWINK

One family I know personally recorded the following effects on members of their family from the time two of them were involved in Masonry;

* Colostomy (bowel &/or stomach removal) - from the oath of the third degree *"let my stomach be removed and burnt to ashes..."*

* Spiritual searching through many religions, including Christian Science, Mormonism, Yoga, Hinduism, Buddhism and many others (any god will do) - the curse from unholy books put "on the level" with God's Word, the Bible.

* Fears - imposed on Freemasons at every degree.

* Adultery and separation - quite prevalent in this family until the curses were broken. Caused by the spiritual adultery/idolatry of having every god "on the level" with the one true God, (Hosea 4:12b, and John 17:3).

* Eyesight confusion - fears of the dark and of light caused by the initiation of the first degree of Entered Apprentice when a blindfold, called a "hoodwink," is imposed on the initiate.

* Heart attack pains and death - from the actions of the first degree with the sharp object placed firmly against the left breast, and also the oath of the second degree for the heart to be ripped out and fed on by wild animals and birds of prey.

* Violence - this is a re-enactment from the third degree, including when the initiate is placed into a coffin.

* Insanity and allergies - these are among the curses imposed by God on those involved in idolatry, (Deuteronomy 28).

In every case mentioned above, when prayers of repentance were made in the name of Jesus Christ, miraculous healings and restorations followed.

Counsellors involved in helping masons and their families to remove the curses and effects of Masonry have noted the following problems which have been healed through prayer in the name of Jesus Christ.

* Allergies (e.g. psoriasis of the skin).

* Alzheimers disease.

* Anger at God.

* Anguish (no peace or rest).

* Angina (from anger).

* Astigmatism (& other eyesight problems).

* Asthma (including hayfever & breathing difficulties).

* Barrenness (inability to conceive, or miscarriages).

47

* Blaspheming (taking God's name in vain).

* Bulimia & Anorexia (based on the death-wish).

* Compulsive risk taking.

* Death wishes, self-destruction and suicide.

* Deceptions through openness to false/non-Christian religions.

* Difficulty in receiving the Baptism in the Holy Spirit or using the gifts (1 Corinthians 12).

* Having a poor relationship with father or stepfather.

* Fears of: death, heart attacks, violent attacks, darkness, light, choking, shame, cancer, man, trusting, the unknown, loud sudden noises, claustrophobia, failure, sickness, rape, betrayal, the supernatural, rejection, panic and many more.

* Heart pains and pains in chest.

* Illegitimacy (leads to difficulty in finding relationship with Father God (see Deuteronomy 23:2).

* Inability to accept Jesus Christ as the **only** way to God.

* Insanity and mental problems.

* Learning disabilities such as Dyslexia, Dyscalculia, Dysgraphia and Dyspore.

* Molestation (both as victim and perpetrator).

* Murderous thoughts.

* Secretiveness (including being unwilling to discuss problems or hurts).

Consider that when prayer offered in the name of Jesus Christ overcomes these and many other problems which have often been traced back to Freemasonry, we begin to realise that the spiritual dimensions of Freemasonry are detrimental to us, as well as being opposed by the God of the Bible. Sometimes there can be other factors (such as involvement in other occultic activity by the individual or their ancestors) but these must be prayed through with competent Christian counsellors. Hereditary curses are the spiritual cause of evil activities which have physical, emotional and spiritual effects passed down through several generations.

Christians should pray for Masons without judging them. Bring their sins to God in an attitude of love, petitioning the Father for His mercy, binding in the name of Jesus Christ the spirits of deception, antichrist, witchcraft and death. Please remember that "**We do not wrestle against flesh and blood** *(your loved one)* **but against principalities, against powers, against the rulers of the darkness of this world, against spiritual wickedness in high places,**" (Ephesians 6:12). This is a spiritual battle, and should be treated accordingly.

Prayer of Release for
Freemasons & their Descendants

If you were once a member of a Masonic organisation or are a descendant of someone who was, we recommend that you pray through this prayer from your heart. Please don't be like the Freemasons who are given their obligations and oaths one line at a time and without prior knowledge of the requirements. Please read it through first so you know what is involved. It is best to pray this aloud with a mature Christian present. We suggest a brief pause following each paragraph to allow the Holy Spirit to show any related issues which may require attention.

A significant number of people also reported having experienced physical and spiritual healings as diverse as long-term headaches, bad backs, nightmares, heart conditions and epilepsy as the result of praying through this prayer. Christian counsellors and pastors in many countries have been using this prayer in ministry and counselling situations for several years, with real and significant results.

Some language could be described as 'quaint Old English' and are the real terms used in the Masonic ritual. The legal renunciation opens the way for spiritual, emotional and physical healing to take place.

There are differences between British Commonwealth Masonry and American & Prince Hall Masonry in the higher degrees. Degrees unique to Americans are marked with this sign "*" at the commencement of each paragraph. Those of British Commonwealth decent shouldn't need to pray through those paragraphs.

"Father God, creator of heaven and earth, I come to you in the name of Jesus Christ your Son. I come as a sinner seeking forgiveness and cleansing from all sins committed against you, and others made in your image. I honour my earthly father and mother and all of my ancestors of flesh and blood, and of the spirit by adoption and godparents, but I utterly turn away from and renounce all their sins. I forgive all my ancestors for the effects of their sins on me and my children. I confess and renounce all of my own sins, known or unknown. I renounce and rebuke Satan and every spiritual power of his affecting me and my family, in the name of Jesus Christ.

True Holy Creator God, in the name of the True Lord Jesus Christ, in accordance with Jude 8-10; Psalm 82:1 and 2 Chronicles 18, I request you to move aside all Celestial Beings, including Principalities, Powers and Rulers, and to forbid them to harass, intimidate or retaliate against me and all participants in this ministry today.

I also ask that you prevent these beings of whatever rank, to not be permitted to send any level of spiritual evil as retaliation against any of those here, or our families, our ministries, or possessions.

I renounce and annul every covenant made with Death by my ancestors or myself, including every agreement made with Sheol, and I renounce the refuge of lies and falsehoods which have been hidden behind.

In the name of the Lord Jesus Christ I renounce and forsake all involvement in Freemasonry or any other lodge, craft or occultism by my ancestors and myself. I also renounce and break the code of silence enforced by Freemasonry and the Occult on my family and me. I renounce and repent of all pride and arrogance which opened the door for the slavery and bondage of Freemasonry to afflict my family and me. I now shut every door of witchcraft and deception operating in my life and seal it closed with the blood of the Lord Jesus Christ. I renounce every covenant, every blood covenant and every alliance with Freemasonry or the spiritual powers behind it made by my family or me. In the name of Jesus Christ, I rebuke, renounce and bind Witchcraft, the principal spirit behind Freemasonry, and I renounce and rebuke Baphomet, the Spirit of Antichrist and also the spirits of Death, and Deception.

I renounce and rebuke the Spirit of Fides, the Roman goddess of Fidelity that seeks to hold all Masonic and occultic participants and their descendants in bondage, and I ask the One True Holy Creator God to give me the gift of Faith to believe in the True Lord Jesus Christ as described in the Word of God.

I also renounce and rebuke the Spirit of Prostitution which the Word of God says has led members of Masonic and other Occultic organisations astray, and caused them to become unfaithful to the One True and Holy God. I now choose to return and become faithful to the God of the Bible, the God of Abraham, Isaac and Jacob, the Father of Jesus Christ, who I now declare is my Lord and Saviour.

I renounce the insecurity, the love of position and power, the love of money, avarice or greed, and the pride which would have led my ancestors into Freemasonry. I renounce all the fears which held them in Freemasonry, especially the fears of death, fears of men, and fears of trusting, in the name of Jesus Christ.

I renounce every position held in the lodge by any of my ancestors or myself, including "Grand Master," "Worshipful Master," or any other occultic title. I renounce the calling of any man "Master," for Jesus Christ is my only master and Lord, and He forbids anyone else having that title. I renounce the entrapping of others into Freemasonry, and observing the helplessness of others during the rituals. I renounce the effects of Masonry passed on to me through any female ancestor who felt distrusted and rejected by her husband as he entered and attended any lodge and refused to tell her of his secret activities. I also renounce all obligations, oaths, curses and iniquities enacted by every female member of my family through any direct membership of all Women's Orders of Freemasonry, the Order of the Eastern Star, or any other Masonic or occultic organisation.

(All participants should now be invited to sincerely carry out in faith the following actions:

(1) Symbolically remove the blindfold (hoodwink) and give it to the Lord for disposal;

(2) In the same way, symbolically remove the veil of mourning, to make way to receive the Joy of the Lord;

(3) Symbolically cut and remove the noose from around the neck, gather it up with the cabletow running down the body and give it all to the Lord for His disposal;

(4) Renounce the false Freemasonry marriage covenant, removing from the 4th finger of the right hand the ring of this false marriage covenant, giving it to the Lord to dispose of it;

(5) Symbolically remove the chains and bondages of Freemasonry from your body;

(6) Symbolically remove all Freemasonry regalia, including collars, gauntlets and armour, especially the Apron with its snake clasp, to make way for the Belt of Truth;

(7) Remove the slipshod slippers to make way for the shoes of the Gospel of Peace;

(8) Symbolically remove the ball and chain from the ankles;

(9) Invite participants to repent of and seek forgiveness for having walked on all unholy ground, including Freemasonry lodges and temples, including any Mormon or any other occultic and Masonic organisations;

(10) Proclaim that Satan and his demons no longer have any legal rights to mislead and manipulate the person seeking help.)

33rd & Supreme Degree

In the name of Jesus Christ I renounce the oaths taken and the curses and iniquities involved in the supreme **Thirty-Third Degree of Freemasonry, the Grand Sovereign Inspector General.** I renounce the secret passwords,

DEMOLAY-HIRUM ABIFF, FREDERICK OF PRUSSIA, MICHA, MACHA, BEALIM, and ADONAI and all their occult and Masonic meaning. I renounce all of the obligations of every Freemasonry degree, and all penalties invoked. I renounce and utterly forsake The Great Architect Of The Universe, who is revealed in the this degree as Lucifer, and his false claim to be the universal fatherhood of God. I reject the Masonic view of deity because it does not square with the revelation of the One True and Holy Creator God of the Bible. I renounce the cable-tow around the neck. I renounce the death wish that the wine drunk from a human skull should turn to poison and the skeleton whose cold arms are invited if the oath of this degree is violated. I renounce the three infamous assassins of their grand master, law, property and religion, and the greed and witchcraft involved in the attempt to manipulate and control the rest of mankind. In the name of God the Father, Jesus Christ the Son, and the Holy Spirit, I renounce and break the curses and iniquities involved in the idolatry, blasphemy, secrecy and deception of Freemasonry at every level. I renounce the Pantheism of the Ancient and Accepted Rite of English and American Freemasonry, and the Atheism of Grand Orient Freemasonry.

I appropriate the Blood of Jesus Christ to cleanse all the consequences of these from my life. I now revoke all previous consent given by any of my ancestors or myself to be deceived.

Blue Lodge

In the name of Jesus Christ I renounce the oaths taken and the curses and iniquities involved in the **First** or **Entered Apprentice Degree,** especially their effects on the throat and tongue. I renounce the Hoodwink blindfold and its effects on spirit, emotions and eyes, including all confusion, fear of the dark, fear of the light, and fear of sudden noises. I renounce the blinding of spiritual truth, the darkness of the soul, the false imagination, condescension and the spirit of poverty caused by the ritual of this degree. I also renounce the usurping of the marriage covenant by the removal of the wedding ring. I renounce the secret word, BOAZ, and it's Masonic meaning. I renounce the serpent clasp on the apron, and the spirit of Python which it brought to squeeze the spiritual life out of me. I renounce the ancient pagan teaching from Babylon and Egypt and the symbolism of the First Tracing Board. I renounce the mixing and mingling of truth and error, the mythology, fabrications and lies taught as truth, and the dishonesty by leaders as to the true understanding of the ritual, and the blasphemy of this degree of Freemasonry. I renounce the breaking of five of God's Ten Commandments during participation in the rituals of the Blue Lodge degrees. I renounce the presentation to every compass direction, for all the Earth is the Lord's, and everything in it.

I renounce the cabletow noose around the neck, the fear of choking and also every spirit causing asthma, hayfever, emphysema or any other breathing difficulty. I renounce the ritual dagger, or the compass point, sword or spear held against the breast, the fear of death by stabbing pain, and the fear of heart attack from this degree, and the absolute secrecy demanded under a witchcraft oath and sealed by kissing the Volume of the Sacred Law. I also renounce kneeling to the false deity known as the Great Architect of the Universe, and humbly ask the One True God to forgive me for this idolatry, in the name of Jesus Christ. I renounce the pride of proven character and good standing required prior to joining Freemasonry, and the resulting self-righteousness of being good enough to stand before God without the need of a saviour. In the name of Jesus Christ I now command healing of my throat, vocal cords, nasal passages, sinus and bronchial tubes, for healing of the speech area, and the release of the Word of God to me and through me and my family.

In the name of Jesus Christ I renounce the oaths taken and the curses and iniquities involved in the **Second** or **Fellow Craft Degree** of Masonry, especially the curses on the heart and chest. I renounce the secret words SHIBBOLETH and JACHIN, and all their Masonic meaning. I renounce the ancient pagan teaching and symbolism of the Second Tracing Board. I renounce the Sign of Reverence to the Generative Principle. I cut off emotional hardness, apathy, indifference, unbelief, and deep anger from me and my family. In the name of Jesus' Christ I now command healing of the chest/lung/heart area, and also for the healing of my emotions, and ask to be made sensitive to the Holy Spirit of God.

In the name of Jesus Christ I renounce the oaths taken and the curses and iniquities involved in the **Third** or **Master Mason Degree**, especially the curses on the stomach and womb area. I renounce the secret words TUBAL CAIN and MAHA BONE, and all that their Masonic meaning. I renounce the ancient pagan teaching and symbolism of the Third Tracing Board used in the ritual. I renounce the Spirit of Death from the blows to the head enacted as ritual murder, the fear of death, false martyrdom, fear of violent gang attack, assault, or rape, and the helplessness of this degree. I renounce the falling

into the coffin or stretcher involved in the ritual of murder. In the name of Jesus Christ I renounce Hiram Abiff, the false saviour of Freemasons revealed in this degree. I renounce the false resurrection of this degree, because only Jesus Christ is the Resurrection and the Life! I also reject the false and pagan view of immortality presented in this degree.

I renounce the pagan ritual of the "Point within a Circle" with all its bondages and phallus worship. I renounce the symbol "G" and its veiled pagan symbolism and bondages. I renounce the occultic mysticism of the black and white mosaic chequered floor with the tessellated boarder and five-pointed blazing star from ancient witchcraft.

I renounce the All-Seeing Third Eye of Freemasonry or Horus in the forehead and its pagan and occult symbolism. I rebuke and reject every spirit of divination which allowed this occult ability to operate. *(Action: put hand over forehead)* I now close that Third eye and all occult ability to see into the spiritual realm, in the name of the Lord Jesus Christ, and put my trust in the Holy Spirit sent by Jesus Christ for all I need to know on spiritual matters. I renounce all false communions taken, all mockery of the redemptive work of Jesus Christ on the cross of Calvary, all unbelief, confusion and depression. I renounce and forsake the lie of Freemasonry that man is not sinful, but merely imperfect, and so can redeem himself through good works. I rejoice that the Bible states that I cannot do a single thing to earn my salvation, but that I can only be saved by grace through faith in Jesus Christ and what He accomplished on the Cross of Calvary.

I renounce all fear of insanity, anguish, death wishes, suicide and death in the name of Jesus Christ. Death was conquered by Jesus Christ, and He alone holds the keys of death and hell, and I rejoice that He holds my life in His hands now. He came to give me life abundantly and eternally, and I believe His promises.

I renounce all anger, hatred, murderous thoughts, revenge, retaliation, spiritual apathy, false religion, all unbelief, especially unbelief in the Holy Bible as God's Word, and all compromise of God's Word. I renounce all spiritual searching into false religions, and all striving to please God. I rest in the knowledge that I have found my Lord and Saviour Jesus Christ, and that He has found me.

In the name of Jesus Christ I now command healing of my stomach, gall bladder, womb, liver, and any other organs of my body affected by Masonry, and I ask for a release of compassion and understanding for me and my family.

York Rite

I renounce and forsake the oaths taken and the curses and iniquities involved in the York Rite Degrees of Masonry. I renounce the **Mark Lodge**, and the mark in the form of squares and angles which marks the person for life. I also reject the jewel or occult talisman which may have been made from this mark sign and worn at lodge meetings;

I renounce and forsake the oaths taken and the curses and iniquities involved in the **Mark Master Degree** with its secret word JOPPA, and its penalty of having the right ear smote or cut off and the curse of permanent deafness, as well as the right hand being chopped off for being an imposter.

I also renounce and forsake the oaths taken and the curses and iniquities involved in the other York Rite Degrees, including **Past Master,** with the penalty of having my tongue split from tip to root;

and of the **Most Excellent Master Degree**, in which the penalty is to have my breast torn open and my heart and vital organs removed and exposed to rot on the dung hill.

Holy Royal Arch Degree

In the name of Jesus Christ, I renounce and forsake the oaths taken and the curses and iniquities involved in the **Holy Royal Arch Degree** especially the oath regarding the removal of the head from the body and the exposing of the brains to the hot sun. I renounce the false secret name of God, JAHBULON, and declare total rejection of all worship of the false pagan gods, Bul or Baal, and On or Osiris. I also renounce the password, AMMI RUHAMAH and its occultic meaning. I renounce the false communion or Eucharist taken in this degree, and all the mockery, scepticism and unbelief about the redemptive work of Jesus Christ on the cross of Calvary. I cut off all these curses and their effects on me and my family in the name of Jesus Christ, and I command healing of the brain and the mind.

I renounce and forsake the oaths taken and the curses and iniquities involved in the **Royal Master Degree** of the York Rite; the **Select Master Degree** with its penalty to have my hands chopped off to the stumps, to have my eyes plucked out from their sockets, and to have my body quartered and thrown among the rubbish of the Temple.

I renounce and forsake the oaths taken and the curses and iniquities involved in the **Super Excellent Master Degree** along with the penalty of having my thumbs cut off, my eyes put out, my body bound in fetters or shackles and brass, and conveyed captive to a strange land; and also of the **Knights or Illustrious Order of the Red Cross,** along with the penalty of having my house torn down and my being hanged on the exposed timbers.

 I renounce the **Knights Templar Degree** and the secret words of KEB RAIOTH, and also **Knights of Malta Degree** and the secret words MAHER-SHALAL-HASH-BAZ.

I renounce the vows taken on a human skull, the crossed swords, and the curse and death wish of Judas of having the head cut off and placed on top of a church spire. I also renounce the unholy communion.

Ancient & Accepted or Scottish Rite (NOTE: in this rite, only the 18th, 30th, 31st 32nd & 33rd degree are operated in British Commonwealth countries.)

* I renounce the oaths taken and the curses, iniquities and penalties involved in the American and Grand Orient Lodges, including of the **Secret Master Degree,** its secret passwords of ADONAI and ZIZA, and their occult meanings. I reject and renounce the worship of the pagan sun god as the Great Source of Light, and the crowning with laurel - sacred to Apollo, and the sign of secrecy in obedience to Horus;

* of the **Perfect Master Degree,** its secret password of MAH-HAH-BONE, and its penalty of being struck to the Earth with a setting maul;

* of the **Intimate Secretary Degree**, its secret passwords of YEVA and JOABERT, and its penalties of having my body dissected, and of having my vital organs cut into pieces and thrown to the beasts of the field, and of the use of the nine-pointed star from the Kabbala and the worship of Phallic energy;

* of the **Provost and Judge Degree**, its secret password of HIRUM-TITO-CIVI-KY, and the penalty of having my nose cut off;

* of the **Intendant of the Building Degree,** of its secret password AKAR-JAI-JAH, and the penalty of having my eyes put out, my body cut in two and exposing my bowels;

* of the **Elected Knights of the Nine Degree,** its secret password NEKAM NAKAH, and its penalty of having my head cut off and stuck on the highest pole in the East;

* of the **Illustrious Elect of Fifteen Degree,** with its secret password ELIGNAM, and its penalties of having my body opened perpendicularly and horizontally, the entrails exposed to the air for eight hours so that flies may prey on them, and for my head to be cut off and placed on a high pinnacle;

* of the **Sublime Knights elect of the Twelve Degree,** its secret password STOLKIN-ADONAI, and its penalty of having my hand cut in two;

* of the **Grand Master Architect Degree,** its secret password RAB-BANAIM, and its penalties;

* of the **Knight of the Ninth Arch of Solomon or Enoch Degree,** its secret password JEHOVAH, it's blasphemous use, its penalty of having my body given to the beasts of the forest as prey, and I also renounce the revelations from the Kabbala in this and subsequent degrees;

* of the **Grand Elect, Perfect and Sublime Mason or Elu Degree,** its secret password MARAH-MAUR-ABREK and IHUH, the penalty of having my body cut open and my bowels given to vultures for food, and I reject the Great Unknowable deity of this degree;

Council of Princes of Jerusalem

* of the **Knights of the East Degree**, its secret password RAPH-O-DOM, and its penalties;

* of the **Prince of Jerusalem Degree,** its secret password TEBET-ADAR, and its penalty of being stripped naked and having my heart pierced with a ritual dagger;

Chapter of the Rose Croix

* of the **Knight of the East and West Degree,** its secret password ABADDON, and its penalty of incurring the severe wrath of the Almighty Creator of Heaven and Earth. I also reject the Tetractys and its representation of the Sephiroth from the Kabbala and its false tree of life. I also reject the false anointing with oil and the proclamation that anyone so anointed is now worthy to open the Book of Seven Seals, because only the Lord Jesus Christ is worthy;

18th Degree

I renounce the oaths taken and the curses, iniquities and penalties involved in the **Eighteenth Degree of Freemasonry, the Most Wise Sovereign Knight of the Pelican and the Eagle and Sovereign Prince Rose Croix of Heredom.** I renounce and reject the false Jesus revealed in this degree

because He doesn't point to the light or the truth since the True Lord Jesus Christ is the Light of the World and the Truth. I renounce and reject the Pelican witchcraft spirit, as well as the occultic influence of the Rosicrucians and the Kabbala in this degree.

I renounce the claim that the death of Jesus Christ was a "dire calamity," and also the deliberate mockery and twisting of the Christian doctrine of the Atonement. I renounce the blasphemy and rejection of the deity of Jesus Christ, and the secret words IGNE NATURA RENOVATUR INTEGRA and its burning. I renounce the mockery of the communion taken in this degree, including a biscuit, salt and white wine.

Council of Kadosh

I renounce the inappropriate use of the title "Kadosh" used in these council degrees because it means "Holy" and it is here used in a unholy way.

* I renounce the oaths taken and the curses, iniquities and penalties involved in the **Grand Pontiff Degree**, its secret password EMMANUEL, and its penalties;

* of the **Grand Master of Symbolic Lodges or Ad Vitum Degree**, its secret passwords JEKSON and STOLKIN, and the penalties invoked, and I also reject the pagan Phoenecian and Hindu deities revealed in this degree;

* of the **Patriarch Noachite or Prussian Knight Degree,** its secret password PELEG, and its penalties;

* of the **Knight of the Royal Axe or Prince of Libanus Degree**, its secret password NOAH-BEZALEEL-SODONIAS, and its penalties;

* of the **Chief of the Tabernacle Degree,** its secret password URIEL-JEHOVAH, and its penalty that I agree the Earth should open up and engulf me up to my neck so I perish, and I also reject the false title of becoming a "Son of Light" in this degree;

* of the **Prince of the Tabernacle Degree,** and its penalty to be stoned to death and have my body left above ground to rot. I also reject the claimed revelation of the mysteries of the Hebrew faith from the Kabbala, and the occultic and pagan Egyptian, Hindu, Mithraic, Dionysian and Orphic mysteries revealed and worshipped in this degree;

* of the **Knight of the Brazen Serpent Degree,** its secret password MOSES-JOHANNES, and its penalty to have my heart eaten by venomous serpents. I also reject the claimed revelation of the mysteries of the Islamic faith, I reject the insulting misquotations from the Koran, and the gift of a white turban in this degree;

* of the **Prince of Mercy Degree,** its secret password GOMEL, JEHOVAH-JACHIN, and its penalty of condemnation and spite by the entire universe. I also reject the claimed revelation of the mysteries of the Christian religion because there are no such mysteries. I reject the Druid trinity of Odin, Frea and Thor revealed in this degree. I also reject the false baptism claimed for the purification of my soul to allow my soul to rejoin the universal soul of Buddhism, as taught in this degree;

* of the **Knight Commander of the Temple Degree,** its secret password SOLOMON, and its penalty of receiving the severest wrath of Almighty God inflicted upon me. I also reject the claimed revelation of the mysteries of Numerology, Astrology and Alchemy and other occult sciences taught in this degree;

* of the **Knight Commander of the Sun,** or **Prince Adept Degree,** its secret password STIBIUM, and its penalties of having my tongue thrust through with a red-hot iron, of my eyes being plucked out, of my senses of smelling and hearing being removed, of having my hands cut off and in that condition to be left for voracious animals to devour me, or executed by lightening from heaven;

* of the **Grand Scottish Knight of Saint Andrew or Patriarch of the Crusades Degree,** its secret password NEKAMAH-FURLAC, and its penalties;

I renounce the oaths taken and the curses and iniquities involved in the **Thirtieth Degree of Masonry, the Grand Knight Kadosh and Knight of the Black and White Eagle**. I renounce the secret passwords, STIBIUM ALKABAR, PHARASH-KOH and all their occult meaning.

Sublime Princes of the Royal Secret

I renounce the oaths taken and the curses and iniquities involved in the **Thirty-First Degree of Masonry, the Grand Inspector Inquisitor Commander**. I renounce all the gods and goddesses of Egypt which are honoured in this degree, including Anubis with the jackal's head, Osiris the Sun god, Isis the sister and wife of Osiris and also the moon goddess. I renounce the Soul of Cheres, the false symbol of immortality, the Chamber of the dead, the false teaching of reincarnation, and the false god, RA, in the name of Jesus Christ.

I renounce the oaths taken and the curses and iniquities involved in the **Thirty-Second Degree of Masonry, the Sublime Prince of the Royal Secret**. I renounce the secret passwords, PHAAL/PHARASH-KOL and all their occultic meaning. I renounce Freemasonry's false trinitarian deity AUM taken from Hinduism, as well as its parts; Brahma the creator, Vishnu the preserver and Shiva the destroyer. I also renounce all the other Hindu deities and beliefs involved in Freemasonry, in the name of Jesus Christ. I renounce the Zoroastrian deity of AHURA-MAZDA, the claimed spirit or source of all light, and the worship with fire, which is an abomination to God, and also the drinking from a human skull in many rites.

Shriners *(Applies only in North America)*

* I renounce the oaths taken and the curses, iniquities and penalties involved in the **Ancient Arabic Order of the Nobles of the Mystic Shrine**. I renounce the piercing of the eyeballs with a three-edged blade, the flaying or scouring of the feet, the madness, and the worship of the false god Allah as the god of our fathers. I renounce the hoodwink, the mock hanging, the mock beheading, the mock drinking of the blood of the victim, the mock dog urinating on the initiate, and the offering of urine as a commemoration.

All other degrees

I renounce all the other oaths taken, the rituals of every other degree and the curses and iniquities invoked. These include the Acacia, Allied Degrees, The Red Cross of Constantine, the Order of the Secret Monitor, and the Masonic Royal Order of Scotland. I renounce all other lodges and secret societies including Prince Hall Freemasonry, Grand Orient Lodges, Mormonism, the Ancient Toltec Rite, The Order of Amaranth, the Royal Order of Jesters, the Manchester Unity Order of Oddfellows and its womens' Order of Rebekah lodges, the Royal Antediluvian Order of Buffaloes, Druids, Foresters, the Loyal Order of Orange, including the Purple and Black Lodges within it, Elks, Moose and Eagles Lodges, the Ku Klux Klan, The Grange, the Woodmen of the World, Riders of the Red Robe, the Knights of Pythias, the Order of the Builders, The Rite of Memphiz and Mitzraim, Ordo Templi Orientis (OTO), Aleister Crowley's Palladium Masonry, the Order of the Golden Key, the Order of Desoms, the Mystic Order of the Veiled Prophets of the Enchanted Realm, the women's Orders of the Eastern Star, of the Ladies Oriental Shrine, and of the White Shrine of Jerusalem, the girls' order of the Daughters of the Eastern Star, the International Orders of Job's Daughters, and of the Rainbow, the boys' Order of De Molay, and the Order of the Constellation of Junior Stars, and every university or college Fraternity or Sorority with Greek and Masonic connections, and their effects on me and all my family.

Lord Jesus, because you want me to be totally free from all occult bondages, I will burn all objects in my possession which connect me with all lodges and occultic organisations, including Masonry, Witchcraft, the Occult and Mormonism, and all regalia, aprons, books of rituals, rings and other jewellery.

I renounce the effects these or other objects of Freemasonry, including the compass and the square, have had on me or my family, and I break all forms of slavery originating from Freemasonry in the name of Jesus Christ.

In the name and authority of Jesus Christ, I break every curse of Freemasonry in my life, including the curses of barrenness, sickness, Arthritic and other muscular and joint infirmities, mind-blinding and poverty, and I rebuke every evil spirit which empowered these curses.

I also renounce, cut off and dissolve in the blood of Jesus Christ every ungodly Soul-Tie I or my ancestors have created with other lodge members or participants in occultic groups and actions, and I ask you to send out ministering angels to gather together all portions of my fragmented soul, to free them from all bondages and to wash them clean in the Blood of Jesus Christ, and then to restore them to wholeness to their rightful place within me. I also ask that You remove from me any parts of any other person's soul which has been deposited within my humanity. Thank you Lord for restoring my soul and sanctifying my spirit.

I renounce and rebuke every evil spirit associated with Freemasonry, Witchcraft , the Occult and all other sins and iniquities. Lord Jesus, I ask you to now set me free from all spiritual and other bondages, in accordance with the many promises of the Bible. In the name of the Lord Jesus Christ, I now take the delegated authority given to me and bind every spirit of sickness, infirmity, curse, affliction, addiction, disease or allergy associated with these sins I have confessed and renounced, including every spirit empowering all iniquities inherited from my family.

I exercise the delegated authority from the Risen Lord Jesus Christ over all lower levels of evil spirits and demons which have been assigned to me, and I command that all such demonic beings are to be bound up into one, to be separated from every part of my humanity, whether perceived to be in the body or trapped in the dimensions, and they are not permitted to transfer power to any other spirits or to call for reinforcements.

I command, in the name of Jesus Christ, for every evil spirit to leave me now, touching or harming no-one, and go to the dry place appointed for you by the Lord Jesus Christ, never to return to me or my family, and I command that you now take all your memories, roots, scars, works, nests and habits with you. I surrender to God's Holy Spirit and to no other spirit all the places in my life where these sins and iniquities have been.

Holy Spirit, I ask that you show me anything else which I need to do or to pray so that I and my family may be totally free from the consequences of the sins of Freemasonry, Witchcraft, Mormonism and all related Paganism and Occultism.

(Pause, while listening to God, and pray as the Holy Spirit leads you.)

Now, dear Father God, I ask humbly for the blood of Jesus Christ, your Son and my Saviour, to cleanse me from all these sins I have confessed and renounced, to cleanse my spirit, my soul, my mind, my emotions and every part of my body which has been affected by these sins, in the name of Jesus Christ. I also command every cell in my body to come into divine order now, and to be healed and made whole as they were designed to by my loving Creator, including restoring all chemical imbalances and neurological functions, controlling all cancerous cells, reversing all degenerative diseases, and I sever the DNA and RNA of any mental or physical diseases or afflictions that came down through my family blood lines. I also ask to receive the perfect love of God which casts out all fear, in the name of the Lord Jesus Christ.

I ask you, Lord, to fill me with your Holy Spirit now according to the promises in your Word. I take to myself the whole armour of God in accordance with Ephesians Chapter Six, and rejoice in its protection as Jesus surrounds me and fills me with His Holy Spirit. I enthrone you, Lord Jesus, in my heart, for you are my Lord and my Saviour, the source of eternal life. Thank you, Father God, for your mercy, your forgiveness and your love, in the name of Jesus Christ, Amen."

Since the above is what needs to be renounced, why would anyone want to join? Copying of this prayer is both permitted and encouraged provided reference is made to Book title, Author, Publisher & web address - www.jubilee-resources.com or www.jubilee.org.nz. *If additional prayer and ministry is required following the above prayer, please contact the publishers shown on page 2, who may refer you to someone closer to you. We have competent counsellors in many countries around the world.*

If you are a lodge member and wish to resign (or demit) we suggest you photocopy this page and send one copy to each lodge you held membership with, and also one copy to your national Grand Lodge.

PETITION FOR WITHDRAWING (Demit)

Lodge No..

Town/City...

Gentlemen:

When initiated into the Entered Apprentice degree, I was induced to swear that, "I will always hele, ever conceal and never reveal any of the secret arts, parts or points of the hidden mysteries of ancient Freemasonry, which have heretofore, may at this time or shall at any future period be communicated to me as such." In my ignorance, and being led line by line, I indulged in the blood oath you required of me.

Now, gentlemen, after having examined the highest documents of the institution of Freemasonry, I have found that the god of Masonry is positively not the God of the Bible. Freemasonry is in no way compatible with the Christian Faith. Being a Christian as I now am, and confessing the Lordship of Jesus Christ as I do, and having learned of the true nature of Freemasonry, I present to you my Petition of Withdrawal.

I renounce my association with and my obligations to the craft of Masonry, without the least equivocation, mental reservation, or self-evasion of mind. For the Word of God says: **"Do not be unequally yoked together with unbelievers. For what fellowship has righteousness with lawlessness? And what communion has light with darkness?"** (2 Corinthians 6:14).

I have no animosity towards you gentlemen, nor any other man in the Lodge. I trust you did not seek to deceive me deliberately, but the teachings of Freemasonry had deceived us both. I no longer desire any Masonic ritual at my funeral. I request that you formally acknowledge this petition in writing as soon as possible.

Respectfully,

Name..

Address..

Date...

REFERENCES

1. Still, "New World Order -the ancient plan of Secret Societies," p. 28.

2. Ward, "Higher Degrees Handbook," p. 25.

3. Waite, "A New Encyclopaedia of Freemasonry."

4. Rice, "Lodges Examined by the Bible," p. 44.

5. "History of the Church," vol. 4, p. 551-2; vol. 5, p. 2.

6. "Liturgy of the Antient & Accepted Scottish Rite of Freemasonry, Part 3, p. 173.

7. Hall, "The Lost Keys of Freemasonry."

8. Wilmhurst, "The Masonic Initiation," p. 3.

9. Coil, "Masonic Encyclopedia," (quoted from Cultwatch, p. 101).

10. Mackey, "Revised Encyclopedia of Freemasonry," vol. 2, p. 847.

11. Higgins, "Ancient Freemasonry," p. 10.

12. Ward, "Freemasonry - its Aims and Ideals," p. 185,

13. Pike, "Morals & Dogma," p. 213.

14. Morey, "The Origins & Teachings of Freemasonry." pp. 115-116

15. Wayne, "Freemasonry - an Interpretation."

16. Ronayne, "Masonic Oaths Null & Void."

17. Taylor, video - "Freemasonry - from Darkness to Light."

18. Pike, "Morals & Dogma," p. 295.

19. Haywood, "The Builder," p. 17.

20. Leadbeater, "The Hidden Life in Freemasonry," p. 131.

21. Ward, "Who is Hiram Abiff," p. 48.

22. Mackey, "Symbolism of Freemasonry," p. 353.

23. Ward, "Entered Apprentice Masonic Handbook," p. vii.

24. Pike, "Morals & Dogma," p. 321

25. Hislop, "The Two Babylons." p. 43.

26. Still, "New World Order -the ancient plan of Secret Societies," p. 31.

27. Button, "Worthy Masons All," p. 20. (Commended by Grand Master, United Lodge of Victoria.)

28. Vindex, "Light Invisible," p. 49. (Anonymous Masonic author who admitted more than he realised.)

29. G.J.O. Moshay "Who is this Allah," pps 134, 135.

30 "Blinded by the Lie" by Rev. Lyndon Ellis, p 144-145.

RECOMMENDED READING

For information about Masonic teaching, history and rituals the following books have been most helpful in my research, and I recommend them for your purchase should you wish to study this important subject deeper. I have used other resources but for space reasons I haven't included what I can't recommend.

"Masonic Rites and Wrongs," by Steven Tsoukalis (P & R Publishing) [One of the best researched books I have read on Masonry, and which came to hand after I had completed the International edition of this book.]

"Blinded by the Lie," by Rev. Lyndon Ellis, Queensland, Australia.

"Freemasonry: the Invisible Cult in our Midst," by Past W. Master Jack Harris

"Armageddon Within," by Past W. Master Jack Harris, (former State Lecturer in Blue Lodge Ritual)

"Darkness Visible," & "Christian By Degrees," by Walton Hannah, (Augustine Publishing)

"Masonic Lodge," by George A Mather & Larry A Nichols, (Zondervan) [Another great little book which arrived after I had completed my research.]

"The Brotherhood," by Stephen Knight, (Grafton/Collins)

"Cult Watch - What you need to know about Spiritual Deception," by John Ankerberg & Dr. John Weldon, (Harvest House)

"New World Order: the Ancient Plan of Secret Societies," by William T Still, (Huntington House)

"The Southern Baptist Convention & Freemasonry," Vols. 1,2 & 3, by Dr. James L Holly, (Mission & Ministry to Men Inc.)

"Heresies Exposed," by Wm. C. Irvine, (Pickering & Inglis)

"Lodges Examined by the Bible," by Dr. John R. Rice (Sword)

"Freemasonry - Friend or Foe?" by Donald A. Prout.

"Freemasonry and Christianity," by Dr. Alva J. McClain, (BMH Books)

"Freemasonry - a Way of Salvation?" by John Lawrence, (Grove)

"Should a Christian be a Mason?" by E.M. Storms (New Puritan Library)

"Evicting Demonic Squatters & Breaking Bondages," by Noel & Phyl Gibson (Freedom in Christ)

"Secret Societies and Subversive Movements," by Nesta H. Webster (Christian Book Club of USA.)

"The Curses and Bondages of Freemasonry," by Kevin Ekert (Australian Christian Ministries) {The author is a former 32° Freemason whole held ranking office in the Grand Lodge of New South Wales.)

"The Bondages of Women in Freemasonry Orders," by Kevin Ekert (Australian Christian Ministries)

Video - "Freemasonry - from Darkness to Light," by Free the Masons Ministries, Issaquah, Washington,

IN SUMMARY

Freemasonry is a religion in its own right, according to its own authorities. There is little in its beliefs which is acceptable to true Christians. This explains why so many Christian denominations oppose Freemasonry. Church attendance should never be confused - or substituted - for a relationship with Jesus Christ. There is an life-changing difference with eternal repercussions. One friend of mine who was a Freemason for 25 years, held Grand Rank and who advanced to the 32° stated, *"It wasn't until I had completely renounced Freemasonry ...and resigned from all my Masonic commitments that I really had fellowship with the Lord Jesus."* People are free to choose, but they cannot be both Freemasons and Christians - these are not compatible.

Any genuine Christian content in Freemasonry was removed 200 years ago. Its blood oaths are blind contracts to commit murder and other crimes of violence, mutilation and deceit. The god of Freemasonry is not the true God who reveals Himself through the Bible. The true and open union of a couple in marriage is prevented because of secrets which Freemasons dare not share with their wives, most of whom would object strongly if they knew what went on. Those in the lower degrees are deliberately deceived by those above them.

Freemasonry holds many people in slavery with a false hope of spiritual, salvation and immortality which emphatically excludes the true Saviour and Lord Jesus Christ. My heart's desire is to see these people released from the curses and iniquities which they have brought on themselves and their families, and for each one of them to find the true freedom, service and brotherhood which can be found only in Jesus Christ and His Church.

Proverbs 14:12 says **"There is a way that seems right to a man but in the end it leads to death."** Freemasonry is a road to spiritual death. Don't expect God to ignore such idolatry. It was Jesus Christ of Nazareth who died for my sins and your sins. Jesus Christ is **"the only Way to God "**(John 14:6 and 1 Timothy 2:4-5) and there is **"no other name under heaven given to mankind by which we must be saved!"** (Acts 4:12). God says that!

If you are a Freemason then I invite you before Almighty God to renounce the idolatry and blasphemy into which you were tricked and deceived. *Please pray through the prayer which commences on page 48.* If any member of your family (regardless of how many generations ago) was ever a Freemason or any of the other groups mentioned, then every member of your family has been placed under a curse or iniquity. In Exodus 20:4-5 God speaks a curse on all who get involved in the worship of false gods. Everyone in your family will require ministry to deal with this. However, I have some good news for you - Jesus Christ has come to set you free, and those He sets free are free indeed! He awaits your decision now.

Resources Available by Dr. Selwyn Stevens

Book Title	*order code*
How to Recognize the Voice of God *	#BHRS
Healing & the Disciples of Jesus Today!*	#BHDS
Treated or Tricked - Alternative Health Therapies Diagnosed *	#BTTB
Insights into Martial Arts/Tai Ch'i/TM/Yoga *	#BMAS
The New Age - Old Lie in a New Package	#BNAS
Dealing with Curses & Iniquities *	#BDWS
Dealing with Demons *	#BDDS
The Bride Made Herself Ready (Spiritual Warfare) *	#BTBS
The Warrior Bride (Spiritual Warfare manual)	#BTWJ
Holy Spirit - Baptism & Filling *	#BHSS
Unmasking Freemasonry - Removing the Hoodwink *	#BFMS
Unmasking Mormonism - Who are the Latter-day Saints? *	#BUMS
Unmasking the Watchtower- Who are Jehovah's Witnesses? *	#BUWS
Unmasking Spiritualism - Supernatural Deceivers	#BUSS
Fatal Faith - Cult Counterfeits of Christianity *	#BFFS
Signs & Symbols & what they mean	#BSSS
Servant of Two Masters - 'Christian' Masons?	#BSTS
Essentials for Faith	#BEFS
Apocalypse Soon: End Times Explained *	#METS
Unveiling the Messiah in the Passover *	#BUTS
To Whom Shall We Go? (World Religions & Christian Mission)	#BTWS
Where Have All The Miracles Gone? "	#BWHS
Insights into Dying, Death & Destinations	#BIDS
This Gospel of the Kingdom *	#BGKS
How to Minister to Change Lives & Communities *	#BHTJ
Raising a Blessed Generation *	#BRAS
Apocalypse Soon: End Times Explained *	#METS
Reversing the Curse on your Finances * (DVD only)	#DRCS
Prophetic Deliverance Training (DVD only)	#DPDT
The Messianic Passover (DVD only)	#DMPS
The Feast of Tabernacles (DVD only)	#DFTS

Titles shown with (*) also available on DVD & many also on CD.

Many also available as E-books.

Order from:
Jubilee Resources International Inc.
PO Box 36-044, Wellington Mail Centre 5045,
New Zealand

Secure Web-shop:
www.jubileeresources.org
www.facebook.com/jubileeresources